SPECIAL NEEDS IN ORDINARY SCHOOLS

General editor: Peter Mittler

Associate editors: Mel Ainscow, Brahm Norwich, Peter Pumfrey
and Sheila Wolfendale

Special Needs in the Primary School

Special Needs in the Primary School

One in Five?

Paul Croll
Diana Moses

CASSELL
London and New York

Cassell

Wellington House   370 Lexington Avenue
125 Strand   New York
London WC2R 0BB   NY 10017-6550

First published 2000

British Library Cataloguing-in-Publication Data
A catalogue record for this book is available from the British Library.

ISBN 0-304-70563-2 (hardback)
      0-304-70564-0 (paperback)

Typeset by Kenneth Burnley in Irby, Wirral, Cheshire.
Printed and bound in Great Britain by TJ International Ltd, Padstow, Cornwall.

Contents

Series editor's foreword

There are several good reasons why this book is relevant to every teacher in all primary schools and should be studied by every special educational needs co-ordinator and headteacher.

First and foremost, it provides a factual account of ways in which primary schools are delivering effective teaching and learning to children experiencing difficulties in benefiting from what schools have to offer. The fact that it is based on solid facts and that it reflects the views and voices of people actually doing the job makes a refreshing change from the more familiar diet of special pleading, exhortation and blame to which primary schools have been exposed for so many years.

The authors have talked to some 300 class teachers of children at Key Stage 2, 48 headteachers and 46 special educational needs co-ordinators and obtained detailed information on just over 2,000 children with a wide range of additional educational needs. The book provides a detailed account of the achievements of teachers in meeting the needs of all their pupils, the obstacles which they face and ways in which they wish to be supported from inside and outside the school. Furthermore, some of the findings are unexpected and force us to re-examine long-held assumptions.

At the same time, we are offered a unique historical perspective because in undertaking this research the team revisited the schools which collaborated with them on a very similar survey carried out in the early 1980s. Consequently, we have a focused history of the changing pattern of provision in the same schools over a period of just under twenty action-packed and highly stressful years. During this time, the quality of provision, already good in the early 1980s, improved substantially but also brought with it a greater awareness of the gap between the needs of children and the capacity of the system to find the resources to meet those needs.

The facts reported in the survey provide the foundations for a realistic but helpful analysis of the dilemmas facing schools today. On the one hand, special needs issues are much more centre-stage than they were twenty years ago at the level of the school and of local and central government. Inclusion in school and in society is the central plank of the government's policy and a wide range of mostly welcome new initiatives have been launched and funded. But the education system as a whole remains fragmented and divisive, judging schools by academic excellence and examination results, publishing league tables which take little account of the social and community contexts within which schools are working, and assuming that a drive to raise standards will reach all children equally.

Despite these constraints and obstacles, what comes through both this and the earlier research is the high level of professional commitment and skill shown by the teaching staff. On such foundations, the prospects for inclusion are more than promising.

PROFESSOR PETER MITTLER
University of Manchester, July 1999

1

Introduction

Children with special educational needs, and the appropriate provision for them in mainstream schools, are of considerable current interest and concern. Ever since the publication of the Warnock Report in 1978 (Department of Education and Science, 1978) it has been thought that as many as one in five of the school-aged population could be regarded as having special educational needs. Special needs have therefore become an inescapable issue for all in education. All teachers and schools meet and attempt to provide for special educational needs as an ordinary part of their work. Provision for special educational needs is virtually the only area in which the role of local education authorities has expanded rather than being curtailed in recent years. Parents too are increasingly involved in the processes of identifying and meeting the special educational needs of their children.

It is perhaps worth considering the extent of the extension of the concept of special educational needs since the Warnock Report. The official title of the Warnock Committee was the 'Committee of Enquiry into the Education of Handicapped Children and Young People'. This in itself draws attention to the traditional notion of 'handicap' which informed thinking on special needs up to that point. Handicapped children made up something under 2% of the school-aged population categorized into one of the ten statutory categories of handicap, and educated, for the most part, in separate special schools. The major innovation of the Warnock Committee was to move away from these statutory categories. These had often simultaneously emphasized what was 'wrong' with children rather than their educational needs and at the same time failed to adequately describe their educational difficulties. In moving away from the categories, the Warnock terminology of 'special needs' placed emphasis on identifying the educational provision children needed. It also extended the concept of special needs away from a small number of handicapped children to a continuum of special need including, perhaps, up to 20% of the school population. This development was broadly welcomed by educationalists concerned with special educational needs and, in a study which was the forerunner of the present research (Croll and Moses, 1985), was shown to match the perceptions of class teachers of the educational needs of their pupils. Nevertheless, it is important to keep the usefulness of all educational conceptualizations under review, and in the chapters that follow we shall consider whether it is still helpful to regard such a high proportion of our young people as 'special'.

Special educational needs have been the focus of a number of central government educational initiatives throughout the 1990s. In particular, the Education Act of 1993 introduced the *Code of Practice on the Identification and Assessment of Special Educational Needs* (Department for Education, 1994) which has provided a framework within which all schools operate their special needs provision. The Register of special educational needs which was a major feature of the Code will be discussed in the next chapter. More recently, the Government published a Green Paper on special educational needs, *Excellence for All Children* (Department for Education and Employment, 1997) as one of its early educational initiatives. Other aspects of educational change have also been highly relevant to special educational needs. Concern over standards of literacy and numeracy and over a 'tail of underachievement' are obviously highly relevant here. Initiatives such as the Numeracy and Literacy Hours, designed to raise educational standards, create many issues for schools attempting to meet special educational needs.

In this book we are concerned with special needs mainly from the perspective of mainstream primary schools and, more specifically, schools with Key Stage 2 (age range 7 to 11) pupils. The study is a unique, large-scale survey of special needs in these schools, across fifteen different local education authorities. It draws on interviews with almost 300 class teachers of Key Stage 2 children, with 48 headteachers and 46 special educational needs co-ordinators in the schools. Detailed information was obtained on the special educational needs of over 2,000 children. The book therefore presents evidence on teacher perceptions of pupils with special educational needs in mainstream Key Stage 2 classrooms and on the policies, organization and patterns of provision for such needs. Information was also gathered on the involvement of support services, contacts with parents and views on the inclusion of pupils with various sorts of special needs in mainstream schools. The study presents an analysis of the prevalence of special needs of various kinds in mainstream schools, the nature of the provision offered to these children, and the issues identified by teachers and headteachers in the area of special needs. It is intended to be relevant both to the practice of identifying and meeting special educational needs in mainstream schools and to the development of appropriate policy and provision in the field. It also explores the complex issue of the relationship between teacher and school practice and broader education policy.

A particularly noteworthy feature of the present study is that it repeats a survey of special educational needs in mainstream primary schools conducted in 1981 and published as *One in Five* (Croll and Moses, 1985). Of the 61 schools in the original survey, 50 were selected to be re-visited in 1998 and 44 of these agreed to take part in the second survey. (Details of the re-selection procedure and the eventual sample of 48 schools are given in the Appendix.) This makes it possible to povide a unique comparison of special educational needs in mainstream primary schools from a period just after the publication of the Warnock Report to the situation approaching the end of the century, and following the major reforms of education throughout the late 1980s and 1990s. Much of the data to be presented in subsequent chapters can be given as exact comparisons between the situation in 1981 and that in 1998. The original study was funded by the then Department of Education and Science and was based at the University of Leicester. The later survey was funded by the Economic and Social Research Council and was based at the University of Reading.

Re-visiting the same schools (and occasionally the same teachers and headteachers) provides a particularly good opportunity to study the educational developments of the past twenty years, especially as they impact on special educational needs. The very high level of co-operation we received from the schools (which was also the case in the earlier survey) gives an assurance that we obtained a representative picture of special educational needs in primary schools. Almost 90% of the original sample agreed to take part, all of the headteachers, 95% of class teachers and all but two of the special educational needs co-ordinators were interviewed. (Further details of response rates in both 1981 and 1998 are in the Appendix.) As well as being invaluable for research purposes, this level of co-operation is also an indication of the level of interest in, and concern over, special educational needs in mainstream schools.

This book is directed at a number of audiences: at policy-makers, teachers, student teachers and other education professionals as well as at academics and others with an interest in education and special educational needs. We particularly want to address areas of relevance to practising teachers, headteachers and special educational needs co-ordinators in mainstream primary schools. The book is based in large part on the perspectives of these professionals, and we see the process of bringing these perspectives together in a systematic fashion as a contribution to the development of professional practice. This view of the professional relevance of studies such as the present one is based on the argument that teaching is not only a practical skill, acquired through experience, but is also a thoughtful and knowledgeable activity, and that pedagogic decisions should be informed by careful analysis and conceptualization, and by extensive empirical evidence.

The evidence that we present here brings together the professional experience and perceptions of a large number of teachers and head-teachers in a way that allows the reader to contextualize their personal views and experience within that of the teaching profession more generally. This partly relates to the traditionally very private nature of teaching as an activity. Teachers rarely see other teachers in action, and heads and others responsible for school policies see little of different ways of doing things in different schools. Part of the value of a study like this is that it can present a range and variety of teacher and school approaches to special educational needs and suggest alternative ways of doing things. Bringing together a wide variety of experiences and perspectives in a systematic way can also offer types of understanding and explanation which are not available on the basis of personal experience or particular case studies. It can consider, for example, the relationship between the assessment of learning difficulties and the overall level of achievement in a school, or the variation between levels of special educational need in schools serving different types of social location. Various models of operation of support services, and the impact of local education authority policies on the provision offered to children, are also best understood through comparisons across large numbers of schools and local education authorities.

In the report of the 1981 survey we emphasized the policy relevance of the study in terms of the importance of establishing whether the assumptions of policy-makers matched the classroom level experience of teachers. The assumptions about the extent of special educational needs contained in the Warnock Report and, later, in the 1981 Education Act, were based on epidemiological evidence and expert opinion. We argued that the correspondence between this evidence and the perceptions that teachers had of the educational needs of their pupils was an important precondition of the effective operation of special needs policies.

In the present book we present a related, but somewhat different, perspective, derived in part from our analysis of the earlier evidence (e.g. Croll and Moses, 1989). What we are doing is to move beyond the dichotomy which sees teachers' practice in terms of the implementation of policy developments, and towards an analysis which sees the day-to-day activities of teachers and schools as a creative element in the education policy-making process. This idea of teachers as 'policy-makers in practice' (Croll, 1996a) draws on the way that the practice of teaching invariably involves demands beyond those which teachers can meet. Teachers are therefore constantly setting priorities and making choices in a way that involves professional discretion. Decisions about, for example, which child should receive extra help, at which point an educational psychologist should be consulted and whether a child should be withdrawn from the regular class, are complex professional choices which cannot be regulated by predetermined criteria. Yet the way in which these choices are made effectively creates special education policy. If, because of common sets of values, similar professional training or the same structural constraints, teachers tend to make similar choices, then a systematic set of variations in educational provision is set up which becomes, in effect, an education policy. Examples of this might be systematic patterns in the types of children who are referred for special schooling, or in the areas of the curriculum where failure leads to a child being regarded as having learning difficulties. In this conception of teachers as policy-makers in practice, teachers are not acting deliberately and consciously to influence policy, in the way that they might do through the teacher unions or through other professional associations. Rather, the common elements of teaching situations influence decision-making in areas of discretion which aggregate into policy directions.

This approach to education policy is related to Archer's 'politics of aggregation', the '. . . sums of individual decisions . . . which constitute the environment of "broad" educational politics . . .' (Archer, 1981). Archer has referred to the influences of this aspect of educational demography as 'the dumb pressure of numbers' (Archer, 1979). In many ways this term is appropriate. The numbers of children on the Register of special educational needs and with Statements of special educational needs constitute a pressure which is a major influence on education policy-making and resource allocation both at school and LEA level. Of course this pressure is not really 'dumb', as special educational needs are not simply 'givens' but are the result of educational decisions and are, in a sense, constructed by schools and the educational system. Nevertheless, they are experienced as fixed constraints, and the aggregate sum of many individual decisions about children's special educational needs influences education policy in a significant manner. In the analysis here we are concerned both to delineate the pressure of numbers and to contribute to an understanding of how it comes about.

The central questions to be considered in the present study are the prevalence of special educational needs of various kinds in mainstream primary schools, the provision made for such needs, and the views of teachers and headteachers on various aspects of special educational needs in primary schools. We shall also be concerned with the impact of patterns of provision, LEA policies and the relationships of schools and various support services. Wherever appropriate, the data to emerge from the present suvey will be compared with that from 1981. This dimension of recent history allows us to consider both the continuities over almost twenty years in the experience of special educational needs in primary schools, and also the extent of change. We can therefore examine a variety of claims concerning the impact of more general education policies on special educational needs over the period, and also consider the relationship between the overall educational context and the situation with regard to special educational needs.

In Chapter 2 we look at the various legislative changes which have impacted on the provision for special educational needs since Warnock. These include developments which are explicitly directed at the field of special needs, and broader educational changes, most notably the introduction of the National Curriculum, which inevitably impact in this area. We also consider some conceptual and theoretical issues underlying the analysis of special educational needs.

Chapter 3 deals with the central question being addressed in the book: the prevalence of special educational needs as seen by Key Stage 2 teachers, their distribution across the school system and the extent of change between 1981 and 1998. This gives the essential foundation for the later discussions of factors associated with variations in prevalence and the organization and management of provision for special educational needs. At the risk of pre-empting later analysis, it should be stated at the outset that, as seen by class teachers, there has been a considerable increase in the prevalence of special needs through the 1980s and 1990s.

Chapter 4 considers the factors associated with patterns of distribution of special educational needs. These include both characteristics of children such as age, gender, ethnicity and reading scores, and characteristics of schools such as overall levels of attainment and the socio-economic circumstances of the families served. This discussion will attempt to look at both influences on the difficulties experienced by children and influences on teachers' perceptions of these difficulties, although these are not always easy to disentangle.

Chapter 5 looks at teachers' and headteachers' views on various aspects of special educational needs in mainstream schools. One aspect of these is that of aetiology: the extent to which difficulties are seen as arising from characteristics of the school and the education system, and the extent to which they are seen as arising from factors internal to the child or associated with the child's family circumstances. A further aspect of teachers' and heads' views to be considered here is that of inclusion: to what extent, and for which children, is a mainstream educational placement rather than a special school placement appropriate? Finally in this chapter we look at teachers' expectations of the extent to which children's problems will be overcome.

The next three chapters move on to the question of the provision made in mainstream primary schools for meeting children's needs. In Chapter 6 the type and level of provision made available to children with special needs within the schools in the study is analysed. Comparisons with data from 1981 show the extent of additional special provision within schools since that date. In addition to the overall statistical data, case studies of the provision made for particular children with differing levels and types of special needs are also presented. In Chapter 7 the ways in which schools organize and deliver their provision for special educational needs are analysed, with a particular emphasis on the role of the special educational needs co-ordinator, a key figure in the operation of the Code of Practice in mainstream schools. There is also an analysis of the ways in which children move between stages of the Register of special educational needs and of the relationships between schools and support services. We conclude the discussion of provision in Chapter 8, which looks at the responsibility of the local education authority for special educational needs, and consider some of the arrangements at LEA level for meeting needs and the impact of these on schools. Changes in the role of the LEA are considered, along with the implications of different approaches to resource allocation. We also consider the complex inter-relationship between the provision of additional resources and the definition of special educational need.

In the final chapter we draw together the data on prevalence and provision, together with a consideration of changes over time. These data are then used to consider the current situation with regard to special educational needs at Key Stage 2 and also to consider some of the problems and issues raised in Chapter 2 and elsewhere. This chapter emphasizes the continuity of problems of special educational needs with other problems of schooling. It also brings into question the value, both for teachers and for children, of continuing to regard something like a quarter of primary-aged pupils as being 'special' with regard to their problems with schooling.

The research which forms the basis for this book is principally our recent, ESRC-funded survey of English primary schools. Much of the fieldwork in schools was conducted by a team of colleagues whose role went far beyond that of conventional interviewer and utilized fully their extensive experience of schools and of educational research. Norma Anderson, Dr Maggie Balshaw, Professor Hilary Constable, Dr Elaine Freeman, Sue Greenaway, and Dr Chris Wilkins all made substantial contributions to the success of the project. We are also grateful to Gill Conian and Sylvia Measures for their help in the management of the project and the preparation of this book. The book also draws on our earlier study, funded by the then Department of Education and Science. We are grateful to our ex-colleagues, Professor Gerald Bernbaum, Co-director of the original study, and Jane Wright, a senior member of the research team, for their contribution to that work. The surveys were only possible because very busy headteachers and teachers were prepared to find time to talk to us. In both surveys there were exceptionally high response rates from schools and teachers and it is this very high level of co-operation which enables us to give a representative and accurate picture of special educational needs in English primary schools. We are very grateful to our colleagues in schools for their co-operation in this work: for the time they made available to us and for the thought and concern that went into their comments.

The data on special educational needs in 1981 which appear in a number of the tables, especially in Chapters 3 and 6, are based on the study reported in *One in Five* (Croll and Moses, 1985). Unless otherwise referenced, any figures for 1981 are based on the survey conducted for that study.

Education policy and the concept of special educational needs

In this chapter we shall outline some of the developments in education policy relevant to special educational needs through the period of the 1980s and 1990s. First, we are concerned with those pieces of legislation and other governmental educational iniatives which are directly and explicitly directed at special educational needs. However, many of the policy changes and educational reforms and innovations of the period, although not explicitly directed towards special educational needs, have considerable implications for this area. We shall also, therefore, consider more general legislative and other developments as they impact on the definition of and provision for special needs. During the 1980s and 1990s the concept of special educational needs has both developed and come to increasing prominence. The concept has been informed by the legislation and other governmentally driven changes, and by developments in educational thinking over the period. Although legislation and other policy documents treat the notion of special educational need as unproblematic, it is in fact a shifting and contested concept involving considerable tensions. Some of the difficulties of conceptualization and definition and their relevance for those providing for special educational needs will also be considered here.

POLICY DEVELOPMENTS IN SPECIAL EDUCATIONAL NEEDS

The starting point for this discussion is the publication of the Warnock Report in 1978 (Department of Education and Science, 1978) and the introduction of the Education Act of 1981, which reflected many of the Warnock recommendations. A key feature of the 1981 Act was the way in which it followed the Warnock Report in abolishing the ten statutory categories of handicap which had dominated the provision for special educational needs since the 1944 Education Act. These categories (blind, partially sighted, deaf, partially hearing, educationally subnormal, epileptic, maladjusted, physically handicapped, speech defect, delicate) were associated mainly with special school provision and applied to less than 2% of the school-aged population. The Warnock Report criticized the way that these categories identified difficulties but did not point towards a solution: '. . . to describe someone as handicapped conveys nothing of the type of educational help and hence provision that is required' (Department of Education and Science, 1978, p. 37). The Act also followed Warnock in suggesting that special educational needs were a continuum which extended well beyond those children who had previously been regarded as handicapped, to encompass many others who needed some form of special or additional provision. The Act did not explicitly address the question of the number of children who might need such provision. However, DES Circular 8/81 (Department of Education and Science, 1981b), which followed the Act, accepted that up to 20% of children can be regarded as having special educational needs.

Although the Act and the Circular covered the full range of special educational needs proposed in Warnock, they also followed the recommendations of the Warnock Report in identifying a much smaller number of children as having needs for special educational provision, who should be protected in law. The Act introduced the idea of a 'multi-professional assessment' of the needs of some children, which would be followed by a 'Statement' of their special educational needs and how they should be met. It was explicit in the Circular that children afforded the 'protection of a statement' were to be effectively those in the previous statutory categories of handicap: 'It is expected that the number will correspond approximately to those children formerly ascertained as handicapped under Section 34 of the 1944 Act' (Department of Education and Science, 1981b, para 9).

The introduction of the Statement of special educational needs was one of the most significant and enduring features of the 1981 Education Act. It maintained the additional 'specialness' of some children within a broad concept of special educational need while, at the same time, putting a new emphasis on the centrality of meeting children's needs rather than categorizing them as handicapped. It also created an enduring tension between the identification of need and the availablity of provision. In principle it was possible to state what a child needed without reference to the provision which was available. However, in practical assessment situations the nature of the potentially available resources seemed certain to influence judgements about needs. A parallel tension between need and provision also occurs for those children who had special educational needs but did not have the protection of a Statement. For these children it was the duty of the school governors to '. . . secure that if any registered pupil has special educational needs the special educational provision that is required for him is made . . .' (Department of Education and Science, 1981a, Section 2(5)). However, a child was to be regarded as having special educational needs if his or her needs went beyond what was ordinarily provided in the school. The nature of educational provision in particular schools, as well as the difficulties children experience, therefore becomes part of the definition of special educational needs. The continuing tensions arising from this relationship will be addressed at a number of points in the following chapters.

As well as the introduction of the broad concept of special needs and of Statements of special educational needs, two issues addressed in the Act which have a continuing relevance are integration and the role of parents. The commitment to integration, to the placement of children with special educational needs in mainstream schools, was a weak one. It was hedged round with qualifications about the efficient use of resources, the educational needs of the child and the educational needs of other children. Nevertheless, it established that mainstream education should be regarded as the norm and that any other sort of placement had to be justified. This ongoing debate will be found in much later education policy documents, with the same tension between the principle of inclusion and the realities of the educational needs of children evident. The Warnock Report had included a chapter entitled, 'Parents as Partners', and the theme of parental involvement was taken up in the legislation. Like integration or inclusion, the theme of parental involvement and parental rights has continued to be an important aspect of ongoing policy developments in the area of special educational needs.

The next major piece of educational legislation that explicitly focused on special educational needs was the Education Act of 1993. In particular, the 1993 Act required the Secretary of State to issue a Code of Practice giving local education authorities and school governing bodies practical guidance on their responsibilities towards all children with special educational needs. The *Code of Practice on the Identification and Assessment of Special Educational Needs* (Department for Education, 1994) was issued in the following year. Unlike previous policy documents on special educational needs, such as the Circulars following the 1981 Act, it gives very considerable detail of recommended procedures, rather than simply laying out the principles and objectives of special educational needs provision. These detailed recommendations are not mandatory. The Education Act requires that those to whom the Code applies should have regard to it; but it does not require them to follow its procedures. However, in practice the Code has been followed virtually universally, certainly in the 48 schools studied as part of this project. In fact, informal and anecdotal evidence, from this project and elsewhere, suggests that almost no teachers and very few headteachers or special educational needs co-ordinators realize that they are not bound by the procedures laid down in the Code of Practice.

Key features of the Code of Practice are the five-stage model for responding to special educational needs, the role of the special educational needs co-ordinator in schools, and the development of Individual Education Plans or IEPs. The details of the five-stage model and the roles of the special educational needs co-ordinator will be considered in later chapters. For the present it is only necessary to note some particular features of the Code. The first is that schools are now given extremely detailed guidance on procedures for assessing and meeting special educational needs. Linked to this introduction of centrally determined (but not mandatory) detail is a very much more explicit and bureaucratized system for documenting special educational needs and the school's response to them. All children who have been identified as having special educational needs are to be put on the Register of special educational needs. There are explicit procedures for moving between stages of the Register. The role of special educational needs co-ordinator was created which included responsibility for the Register and other aspects of record keeping.

The Code of Practice maintains the distinction between the most serious forms of special educational needs and other children for whom some sort of special provision should be made. Stage 5 of the Code of Practice is the point when children have the Statement of special educational needs introduced by the 1981 legislation. There is therefore a continuity in these new procedures with the 1981 Act and, through it, with the 1944 legislation and the categories of handicap. However, the detailed procedures and records kept for statemented children are now extended, to some degree, to all children with special educational needs. For the first time all children across the spectrum of special needs are to be formally identified. Therefore, the 1993 Act formalizes and bureaucratizes the extension of the concept of special educational needs contained in the Warnock Report and the 1981 legislation.

A further aspect of the Code of Practice is the development of Individual Education Plans for all children at Stage 2 and beyond. This identifies a highly *individualized* pattern of provision for these children, which has implications for teaching but also is potentially at odds with other current pedagogic developments which stress the common educational needs of children.

As with the earlier legislation, the 1993 Act places considerable emphasis on the roles and rights of parents. These are built into the Code of Practice, with formal parental consultation at all stages. However, the Act also goes further than this in establishing a Special Educational Needs Tribunal where parents can appeal against LEA decisions on assessments and Statements. The Special Educational Needs Tribunal is mainly concerned with the most severe end of the range of special educational needs and has so far had limited impact on special needs in mainstream schools. But it introduces a quasi-judicial element into provision for special educational needs and re-emphasizes the importance of correct bureaucratic procedures and appropriate parental consultation (Special Educational Needs Tribunal, 1995).

There has been no major legislation with regard to special educational needs since the 1993 Act, but the new Labour government has developed a number of policy initiatives on special needs, as elsewhere in education. The Green Paper, *Excellence for All Children: Meeting Special Educational Needs* (Department for Education and Employment, 1997) was followed by *Meeting Special Educational Needs: A Programme of Action* (Department for Education and Employment, 1998). These documents link the development of special needs policies more explicitly to that of other education policies than has been the case with earlier initiatives and legislation. However, in other respects the policy proposals seem very similar to those of previous governments. As before there is a strong commitment to the principle of inclusion (as 'integration' has now become), but with the usual conditions concerning parental choice, the needs of the child and the needs of other children in mainstream schools. The role of parents is reaffirmed with proposals for further partnership schemes and possible changes in the way the Special Educational Needs Tribunal works. Staff development in the area of special educational needs is to be a priority, as is early intervention and prevention strategies. Although the documents claim that they want to 'shift the focus . . . from procedures to practical support' (Department for Education and Employment, 1998, p. 8), it is unclear what this practical support will be.

There are two features of the Green Paper and the *Programme of Action* which are particularly relevant to some of the issues to be presented in this book. The first is the suggestion in the *Programme of Action* document that there may be too many children identified as having special educational needs, and that some children at Stage 1 of the Code of Practice do not have 'real' special needs. This is put tentatively in the *Programme of Action* and raises many issues about the nature of special needs which will re-occur throughout the present study. The second feature of interest is the tension, never explicitly recognized but very apparent in the documents, between the provision for the many children embraced by the 'broad concept' of special educational needs and provision for the relatively few children whose difficulties require resources beyond the school and which call for the intervention of specialist agencies. Most of the discussion in these policy documents is about procedures which are only appropriate for a small proportion of the total of children with special educational needs. For example, the arguments about inclusion and the role of special schools, the Special Educational Needs Tribunals and multi-agency working are irrelevant to most of the children who will be on the Register of special educational needs under the new arrangements. Yet these issues, although they are only relevant to a few children, are so important and so complex that they inevitably dominate policy papers and other government documents. This is a further aspect of the relationship between special and ordinary educational provision which we discuss below.

THE IMPACT OF EDUCATION POLICY ON SPECIAL EDUCATIONAL NEEDS

The period of the 1980s and 1990s, which was the focus of the discussion above, saw many changes and reforms in education policy and practice in addition to those explicitly directed at special educational needs. When something like one child in five is regarded as having special educational needs, it is inevitable that these changes will have both intended and unintended consequences in the area of special education. Some of the relevant educational policies include the introduction of the National Curriculum and its associated assessment arrangements, the publication of 'league tables' of schools' results on National Curriculum assessments, local management of schools and devolved funding, and the encouragement of parental choice and a competitive climate in education.

The introduction of the National Curriculum in the Education Act of 1988 was the most prominent of the educational changes of the period, in that it broke with tradition in giving a centralized prescription of curriculum content. It is an area where there has been a wide disparity between claims over the benefits the National Curriculum brings to children with special educational needs and the educational problems it creates. The initial presentation of the

National Curriculum by the Department for Education and the National Curriculum Council (NCC) strongly emphasized the notion of all children having an entitlement to the full curriculum and explicitly included children with special educational needs in this entitlement. The NCC document on special educational needs in the National Curriculum was entitled *A Curriculum for All* (National Curriculum Council, 1989) and a Special Educational Needs Task Group was established to facilitate access to the National Curriculum for children with special educational needs. There was a number of arguments put forward regarding the benefits of the National Curriculum for children with special educational needs. These included the view that such children sometimes had an unduly restricted curriculum experience and needed guaranteed access to a 'broad and balanced' curriculum. It was also claimed that the structured programmes of study and assessment would prevent difficulties being missed and would allow progress to be assessed. More critical responses to the National Curriculum suggested that aspects of content were inappropriate for children with special educational needs and that the assessment arrangements would be stigmatizing and demotivating for children likely to perform poorly on such assessments. There was also concern that the increased pressure on teachers would lead to less time being available for children with special needs.

A study of primary schoolteachers conducted in the early years of the introduction of the National Curriculum showed a mixed pattern of response, although one in which difficulties tended to predominate (Croll, 1996b). Teachers were initially quite positive about the relevance of the National Curriculum to the needs of their pupils, but became less positive with experience. Teachers who had classes in which they identified a high proportion of children with learning difficulties were considerably less positive than other teachers. While many teachers said that more structured curriculum aims and assessments could help them meet special educational needs, a more common response was that pressures of time, along with pressures to concentrate on the whole class and the class average, would disadvantage such children. The study also highlighted the curriculum difficulties faced by teachers and schools in the area of special needs. The National Curriculum attempts to offer a 'broad and balanced' curriculum to all pupils: but many teachers argued that pupils with learning difficulties needed to focus on basic skills, even though this narrowed their curriculum experience.

Along with the introduction of the National Curriculum came a series of other changes with regard to the management of schools.

These included a greater degree of parental choice, informed by the publication of the results of National Curriculum assessments in a 'league table' format. This, together with the devolution of budgets to schools, led to concerns that some children with special educational needs would become unwelcome in schools concerned with their assessment results and their attractiveness to parents. Gewirtz *et al.* (1995) give examples of schools which were concerned that their reputation for being 'good with special needs children' would lead to them attracting more such children and becoming less attractive to most parents. While there is no systematic evidence of this process operating on a larger scale, the competitive ethos in education engendered by comparisons of test results, and the declining role of the local education authority, provides a potentially difficult climate in which to cater for special needs.

The reduction in the role of LEAs in the governance of education, which has been a feature of education policy in the 1980s and 1990s, has had paradoxical consequences for special educational provision. Alongside this reduction in the LEA role there has been a considerable increase in legal and bureaucratic requirements in the field of special educational needs. Such responsibilities have been less likely to be devolved than responsibilities in other areas of education. Therefore, as the responsibilities of LEAs shrink, special educational needs comes to be a larger and larger part of those remaining, and assumes an increasing prominence in LEA activity (Croll and Moses, 1998). The devolution to schools of budgetary responsibilities for special educational needs which has occurred also has implications beyond those of finance and management. As will be shown in more detail in later chapters, the way that the definition of special needs is related to the availability of resources to meet them creates conceptual issues of what is ordinary and what is special when resources are ordinarily available in schools.

The place of special needs within an educational agenda which is focused on raising standards, especially standards in the basic skills, across the educational system generally, is unresolved within current education policy-making. Many recent government initiatives are claimed to be directed towards improving standards and, as we have seen above, there have been parallel initiatives in the area of special educational needs. But, except at the most general level of all being concerned with 'improvement', there is no relationship between these initiatives and no sense of the extent to which meeting special educational needs and raising overall levels of performance are distinct or overlapping issues. Some of the current initiatives, such as the

Education Action Zones (Department for Education and Employment, 1999), relate, at least in part, to the well-established association between low achievement and poverty. Evidence on the connection between poverty and special educational needs will be discussed in Chapter 4 of this book. Other initiatives are focused on teaching methods within mainstream classrooms. This is particularly so of the Literacy Hour and Numeracy Hour (OFSTED, 1998a, 1998b).

The Literacy and Numeracy Projects raise particular issues for the relationship between low achievement and special educational needs. The areas of the curriculum which they address are, as the evidence presented in Chapter 3 will show, the central and defining issues for special educational needs in mainstream primary schools. Nearly all children regarded by their schools as having special needs are failing in one or both of these areas, most commonly that of literacy. However, a key feature of these projects is that the strategies they introduce are general strategies in which the central feature of the approach is work with the whole class. This raises a question which we shall return to at a number of points in this book, and which concerns many of the teachers we talked to, of whether some children's needs are appropriately regarded as the same or as different from other pupils. Early evaluations of the Literacy and Numeracy Hours have claimed that they are, in general, successful in raising standards of achievement in some very specific aspects of performance (OFSTED, 1998a, 1998b). However, in these reports the results seem to have been less positive in the case of children with special educational needs, especially in the area of literacy.

THE CONCEPT OF SPECIAL EDUCATIONAL NEEDS

Even from the limited discussion so far it is clear that the concept of special educational needs is not as straightforward as it first appears. The idea that this is a concept that can be unambiguously used to describe what children need educationally and that special needs provision represents an attempt to meet these needs is a tempting one. But it disappears beneath the complex interplay of difficulties of definition and conceptualization and the contested nature of special provision. These difficulties will resonate through the presentation of the research results which follow and we shall return to them in the final chapter. The present discussion is intended to sketch out some of the issues surrounding the concept of special educational needs.

Difficulties of this kind have always existed in the field of special education but the broad concept of special educational need,

introduced in the Warnock Report, both brings them to greater prominence and emphasizes their continuity with broader educational
issues. Problems that relate to the education of 2% of children can be
more easily (though not necessarily appropriately) separated off from
general educational debates than can problems relating to the
education of 20% or 25% of the school population.

Once we see the notion of special needs as a continuum extending
widely into the school population, definitional problems become particularly acute. Between the obvious specialness of every individual
child and the obvious extreme difficulties experienced by a small
minority, it is very hard to define a point at which educational needs
become special. This was particularly apparent when we looked at the
relevance of broader educational policies to special educational needs.
A concern to raise standards overall, with a particular focus on
reducing levels of under-achievement or low achievement, must
inevitably focus on children with special educational needs, especially
so when a significant minority of pupils are regarded as having such
needs. Put like this, addressing problems of low achievement is the
same as meeting and even reducing special educational needs. But the
definition of special educational needs in the Code of Practice – '. . .
significantly greater difficulty in learning than that of the majority of
children of the same age' (Department for Education, 1994) – makes
special needs, or at least learning difficulties, relative to the performance of other pupils. So if initiatives designed to improve
performance overall are successful, they might still leave the same
number of pupils being regarded as having special needs if they were
still performing less well than their peers, albeit at a higher overall
level. We would not want to over-emphasize this relativistic aspect of
special needs when there is no doubt that many children are experiencing serious difficulties in learning and other aspects of schooling.
But the conceptual difficulties it creates are unavoidable, especially
when considering what proportion of the school population can
properly be regarded as having special educational needs.

Associated with the broad concept of special educational needs
introduced in the Warnock Report is the move away from categories
of special need: of classifying children by their handicaps or what was
assumed to be 'wrong' with them. Although categorization has disappeared formally, we have commented elsewhere (Croll and Moses,
1999) that there is a very considerable continuity over time in the
descriptions applied to pupils and the provision made for them. In the
present study it emerges clearly that, although the terminology used
to describe children and provision has changed over time, it can be

mapped very readily onto earlier usage. This is not surprising, as changes in terminology and the end of categories do not in themselves change the difficulties children and their schools experience.

In our earlier study we commented on the perspectives on special educational needs which stressed the ways in which such needs were socially constructed, and which emphasized the roles these constructs played, other than those of helping children. In this discussion we wanted to make it clear that special educational needs are a socially constructed category, just as any categories or definitions used in education and elsewhere in the social world are socially constructed. However, to see them in this way is not to say that their application is arbitary or that that they have in some sense been invented by the educational system. In 1985 we argued that '. . . the fact that categories of special need are socially created and that the application of them to individual children is imperfect does not mean that difficulties to which they refer are not real' (Croll and Moses, 1985, p. 20). More recently, authors such as Clark, Dyson and Millward (1998), while recognizing that special educational needs are socially produced, also argue that '. . . although categories may be constructed they are not entirely arbitrary. Once education . . . brings about differential responses from students . . . [w]hether teachers, and other education professionals choose on the basis of these differential responses, to construct categories of students or not the differences themselves remain' (p. 168). These authors also show how the 'new paradigm' of studies of special educational needs (for example, Barton, 1988; Slee, 1993; Fulcher, 1989) pays very little attention to the empirical study of schooling. This echoes our earlier critique of some sociological accounts of special education which, in drawing attention to the latent social and institutional functions served by special needs provision, ignore their manifest functions of offering services to children.

A useful way of considering the complex and value-laden issues surrounding special educational needs is in terms of a set of dilemmas, as proposed by Norwich (1993). Drawing on the work of Minow (1985) in the United States he identifies the 'difference dilemma': 'How can schools deal with children defined as different without stigmatising them on that basis?' This addresses a theme running through the discussion above: special educational provision is designed to respond to the needs of children but it is frequently regarded as problematic for them and sometimes as a negative educational experience. Norwich identifies four dimensions along which dilemmas arise in special educational needs. The *curriculum* dilemma relates to the tension between seeing all children as having the same curriculum entitlement but also seeing some children as having different curriculum needs. This dilemma relates to the problems the introduction of the National Curriculum created for provision for special needs. The *identification* dilemma relates to the tension between the need to assess and identify children whose needs may be different and the danger that such identification may be stigmatizing or self-fulfilling. Some of these questions arise with regard to the use of categories discussed above. The *integration* dilemma relates to the placement of pupils and the tension between the widespread preference in principle for all children to be educated along with their peers and the very specialist provision some children need. The *parent–professional* dilemma relates to the recognition of the importance of parental rights and parental preferences which may conflict with professional judgements about what is appropriate for a child. In an empirical study of the views of education professionals in the United Kingdom and the United States, Norwich found that both groups recognized the first three dilemmas as arising in their work, but that they were much less likely to recognize the parent–professional dilemma.

The notion of dilemmas helps to focus on the enduring nature of some of the issues in special educational needs, and also on the way in which these are inextricably locked into wider features, not only of particular educational systems, but of the process of education more generally. A useful related discussion can be found in Clark *et al.* (1998). But in seeing special needs in terms of dilemmas and in recognizing the heavily value-laden nature of issues in special educational needs, we should not lose sight of the importance of empirical evidence from specific educational contexts in further understanding such issues and moving forward policy and practice.

We argued in the previous chapter that part of the value of a survey of the kind reported here is that it enables teachers and headteachers to locate their own experiences and perspectives within a wider context. The wider context of the nature of the special educational needs of children and their schools' responses to them are also relevant to the definitional and conceptual issues discussed above. In the absence of fixed and objective criteria for special educational needs, the situation with regard to special needs is created by the interplay between the difficulties of children and the responses of their schools. Many of the issues discussed above relate crucially to the actions and perceptions of education professionals. The way that schools and teachers see special educational needs is a key part of implementing and developing policy on special needs, but is also an element in understanding these needs.

The nature and extent of special educational needs in mainstream classrooms

A key question for any discussion of policy and practice in the field of special educational needs is that of prevalence: how many children are we talking about, where are they to be found and what is the nature of their special educational needs? As we saw earlier, the Warnock Report suggested that as many as one child in five could be regarded as having special educational needs. This contrasted with the figure of approximately one child in 50 formally classified as handicapped at the time of the Report and the approximately one child in 40 with a Statement of special educational needs at the time of writing.

In our earlier study of special educational needs in the primary school it was argued that it was crucial to establish the degree of match between the assumptions about prevalence made by policy-makers and the perceptions of special educational needs of teachers based on immediate classroom experience. That study showed a fairly close match. When classroom teachers of what are now Key Stage 2 pupils were asked about children in their classes who had special educational needs they identified, on average, just under 20%. This corresponded with the assumptions in the Warnock Report and the 1981 legislation that between one in five and one in six children had special educational needs. It is important to note that teachers in that study were not asked to estimate how many children in general had special educational needs, but were asked about specific children in their classes. It was the aggregate from this procedure, not generalized estimates, that matched the policy assumptions at the time.

In the context of the Code of Practice, and the many other developments in provision for special educational needs discussed in Chapter 2, the extent of the match between teacher perceptions and policy assumptions is, if anything, even more crucial than it was in the early 1980s. As we have seen, procedures for identifying, recording and providing for special educational needs have become very much more formalized and bureaucratic through the 1980s and 1990s. They have also become very much more dominated by procedures for accessing and accounting for resources. But despite this increased formality and explicitness, the central role played by the class teacher's experience of the child in the classroom has remained. As a context for any consideration of the operation of the Code of Practice, Individual Education Plans and procedures for allocating resources, we need a view of special educational needs as seen by classroom teachers.

SPECIAL EDUCATIONAL NEEDS IN 1981 AND 1998: AN OVERVIEW

The survey carried out in 1981 involved interviews with 428 teachers of junior-age (Key Stage 2) classes in 61 randomly selected schools in ten different local education authorities. In 1998, 48 schools, 44 of them from the original sample, took part in the follow-up study. (Full details of the sampling and response rates are given in the Appendix.) The 1998 figures are based on interviews with 285 teachers in 46 schools. The substantial sample size, the involvement of the same schools and, in particular, the very high response rate from both schools and teachers, provides a secure base both for a picture of the prevalence of different sorts of special educational needs and for the change in such prevalence over time.

In 1981 teachers were initially asked to describe any children in their classes who they regarded as having special educational needs. They were then prompted further with a set of types of special needs. However, over 90% of the children described by teachers were nominated in response to the initial general question. In 1998 teachers were asked initially about children who were on the Register of special educational needs. They were then asked if there were other children in their class who they regarded as having special educational needs, but hardly any additional children were nominated.

Table 3.1 gives an overview of special educational needs in mainstream Key Stage 2 classrooms based on interviews with class teachers. In 1981 there was a total of 12,310 pupils in the classrooms studied; of these, 2,317 or 18.8% were regarded by their teachers as having special educational needs. This result supported the view of the Warnock Committee that special educational needs should be seen as a continuum extending well into the mainstream school system. It also supported the Warnock estimate that between one in five and one in six children had some form of special educational needs. In the 1998 survey 285 teachers were interviewed about pupils in their classes with special educational needs. Of the 8,149 pupils in these class-rooms, 2,123 or 26.1% were described by their teachers as having special educational needs. Nearly all of these children were on the special educational needs Register. As Table 3.1 shows, in the seventeen years from 1981 to 1998 the proportion of pupils within this age range regarded by their teachers as having special educational needs had increased from 18.8% to 26.1%: an increase of 38.8% on the 1981 baseline.

Table 3.1: Special educational needs 1981–98: an overview

	1998			1981			% change 1998–81
	N	% of all pupils	% of CSEN	N	% of all pupils	% of CSEN	
All SEN	2,123	26.1	100.0	2,317	18.8	100.0	+38.8
Learning difficulties	1,884	23.1	88.7	1,898	15.4	81.9	+50.0
Emotional and behavioural difficulties	756	9.3	35.6	953	7.7	41.1	+20.8
(discipline problems*)	422	5.2	19.9	500	4.1	21.6	+26.8
Health, sensory and physical difficulties	352	4.3	16.6	540	4.5	23.3	−4.0
N =		8,149	2,123		12,310	2,317	

* Also included in 'emotional and behavioural difficulties'

The causes of this quite striking increase are likely to be varied and complex. In particular, the extent of real changes in the educational needs of children, changes in teacher perceptions, changes in cur-riculum and pedagogy in schools, changes in procedures for identifying special educational needs and the interplay between these may all be relevant. Some issues relating to this have already been touched on in Chapters 1 and 2. In the rest of this chapter we shall be looking in more detail at characteristics of children with special edu-cational needs and changes in these over time. In Chapter 4 we shall look in more detail at some of the evidence regarding different groups of children and different levels of achievement associated with special educational needs.

In the 1998 survey detailed information was gathered regarding the nature of the difficulties that led to a pupil being regarded as having special educational needs. These data will be discussed later in this chapter. For the purposes of this overview, and for comparison with 1981, special educational needs have been grouped into three broad categories. First, any needs directly associated with learning, including all-round learning difficulties and various sorts of specific difficulties, have been grouped together. Second, any needs associated with behaviour or emotional development, including, but not exclusively, discipline problems, have been put together. Third, any needs associated with physical disabilities, health problems or sensory difficulties have been classified together. These broad groupings or major categories are directly comparable with the data obtained in 1981, and the two sets of figures are presented together in Table 3.1. There is, of course, a good deal of overlap between the groupings, with many children described as being in more than one of the broad categories of special needs.

In 1981 difficulties with learning were by far the largest of the major categories of special educational needs. The proportion of all pupils described as having learning difficulties was 15.4% and these children made up 81.9% of all children with special educational needs. This predominance of learning difficulties was even greater in 1998, with 23.1% of all pupils being described as having learning difficulties and 88.7% of all children with special needs being described in this way. The proportion of pupils in mainstream primary schools with learning difficulties had increased by exactly 50% between 1981 and 1998.

There was also an increase in the proportion of children with emotional and behavioural difficulties but not to the same extent as for learning difficulties. In 1981 7.7% of pupils were described as having emotional or behavioural difficulties. These children made up 41.1% of all those with special educational needs. In 1998 the proportion had risen to 9.3%. This was an increase of 20.8% from the 1981 baseline, an increase of less than half the increase in learning difficulties. Although there is an increase overall, because of the much greater increase in learning difficulties, children with emotional and behavioural difficulties make up a smaller proportion of all those with special educational needs than in 1981.

Included within the major category 'emotional and behavioural difficulties' were children described as presenting discipline problems in the classroom. Most of the more detailed analysis of particular categories will be presented later in this chapter. However, because of the considerable current concern about increases in problem behaviour and pupil exclusion from school, discipline problems are included in this overview. In 1981, 4.1% of pupils were described by their teachers as presenting them with problems of classroom discipline. In 1998 this figure was 5.2%, an increase of 26.8% on the 1981 baseline. Although this is a substantial increase it is still relatively small in absolute terms (an increase of about one child in 100) and it is a considerably smaller percentage increase than the increase in special educational needs overall.

The third major category was 'health, sensory and physical difficulties'. Unlike the trend for special educational needs overall, there has been no increase in the prevalence of such difficulties between the two surveys. In 1981, 4.5% of all pupils were regarded by their teacher as having such difficulties and this amounted to 23.3% of all children with special educational needs. In 1998, 4.3% of pupils were described by their teachers in this way, a small decrease from the 1981 baseline. These children made up 16.6% of all those with special educational needs in 1998, a decrease from just under a quarter in 1981. As the overall proportion of children regarded as having special educational needs increased, the absence of such an increase in health, sensory and physical difficulties means that they make up a substantially smaller proportion of all those with special educational needs, even though the absolute level has only gone down very slightly.

It is immediately evident from the figures in Table 3.1 that both in 1981 and1998 there was a considerable overlap between the major categories of special educational need. A substantial proportion of the children who appear in each category also appear in other categories. In Table 3.2 details are provided of the overlap between categories. The figures show that in 1998 7.1% of pupils had both learning and emotional and behavioural difficulties; 3.6% of pupils had both learning difficulties and physical, sensory or health problems and 1.7% of pupils had both physical, sensory or health problems and emotional or behavioural difficulties. Included in these figures are 1.4% of pupils in all three categories. Most of these figures show a small increase compared to 1981 as proportions of the total pupil population. However, because the total number of children with special needs has increased, they show a small decrease as proportions of this population.

The very different proportions of children in the three major categories means that the association between difficulties is assymetrical. In particular, of the children with learning difficulties of some kind, 30.1% also have emotional or behavioural problems and 15.8% also have physical, sensory or health problems. In contrast, of the children with emotional or behavioural problems, 76.4% also have learning difficulties. And of the children with physical, health or sensory problems, 84.3% also have learning problems. Partly because of the predominance of learning difficulties in special educational needs, even greater in 1998 than in 1981, children with other sorts of special educational needs often also have learning difficulties. In many cases these difficulties, both those related to health and those related to behaviour, may be responsible for learning difficulties. But also, in the case of emotional and behavioural difficulties, frustration at difficulties with learning may lead to other problems. Some evidence on teacher perceptions of these relationships will be discussed in Chapter 5.

Table 3.2: Special educational needs 1981–98: overlap between major categories

	1998		1981	
	% of CSEN	% of all pupils	% of CSEN	% of all pupils
Learning difficulty and EBD	7.1	27.2	5.3	28.1
Learning difficulty and physical/ sensory/medical difficulty	3.6	14.0	2.9	15.3
Physical/sensory/ medical difficulty and EBD	1.7	6.6	1.8	9.5
All major categories*	1.4	5.6	1.2	6.5
N =	2,123	8,149	2,317	12,310

* Also included in the other rows of the table

It is clear from the summary data presented so far that in 1998 a very substantially greater proportion of pupils were being placed on the Register of special educational needs than the proportion regarded by their teachers as having special educational needs in 1981. These figures match the most recent data available from OFSTED and DfEE which show a similar increase in numbers on the Register of special educational needs. The figures also confirm the perceptions of the headteachers interviewed in the present study. In these interviews headteachers were asked whether they thought the proportion of children in their school with special educational needs had changed since 1980, or since the most recent point they could judge from. 60% of the headteachers said that the extent of special educational needs had increased over this period and only one out of the 48 headteachers said that special educational needs had decreased. Of those saying that the prevalence of special educational needs had increased, about a third accounted for this in terms of changes in the catchment area served by the school. These heads were saying that the increase had come about as a result of changes in the characteristics of their pupils associated with social changes in the neighbourhood. On the other hand, half accounted for the increase in terms of changed procedures for identifying and recording special needs. These heads were saying that the increase was a consequence, not of changes in the children served by the school, but changes in the way that the school viewed them. No headteacher said that changes in the prevalence of special educational needs was a consequence of other educational developments such as the introduction of the National Curriculum or changes in the management of schools.

Whatever factors are responsible for the increase, it cannot be accounted for by the movement towards the inclusion of children with special educational needs in mainstream settings rather than in segregated special schools. There has been some progress in inclusion or integration since 1981, but it has been slow and uneven and the number of children involved is only a very small percentage of children with special needs in mainstream schools. The decrease in the special school population has been at the most about 0.5% of the total school population and could only have a tiny impact on the figures reported here (see, e.g., Norwich, 1997).

What is very apparent from the changes in prevalence of special educational needs is the increased predominance of learning difficulties. Learning difficulties dominated teacher perceptions of special educational needs in 1981 and did so to an even greater extent in 1998. The increase in the proportions of children regarded as having learning difficulties is 50%, a growth of more than double that of any other category of special educational needs. It is particularly striking that the increase in the broad category of emotional and behavioural difficulties and also in the specific category of discipline problems is much less than that for learning difficulties. Despite the considerable public debate about children's emotional and behavioural development, the concern about increasing levels of exclusion from school and the increase in special school provision for pupils with emotional and behavioural difficulties, there has only been a relatively small increase in teacher perceptions of these difficulties at the level of the classroom.

In Chapter 4 we shall look at the levels of achievement associated with being regarded by teachers as having learning difficulties and compare these for 1998 and 1981. This will help throw light on factors underlying the apparent considerable increase in such difficulties. With regard to the debates over the National Curriculum discussed in Chapter 2, the present figures give at least tentative support to the argument reported there that it would impact negatively on the education of children with difficulties. However, this was not the explanation offered by the headteachers interviewed.

SPECIAL EDUCATIONAL NEEDS ACROSS CLASSROOMS AND SCHOOLS

The figures discussed so far have been aggregated across the 46 schools and 285 classes involved in this part of the study. However, in addition to the question of the overall prevalence of special educational needs and the change in such prevalence over time, is the question of the way in which special educational needs are distributed across schools and classrooms. There are strong reasons to expect that schools will vary with regard to their experience of special educational needs. There is a very well-established relationship between the social circumstances of children and their families, and especially the material disadvantages associated with poverty, and educational performance, health and personal adjustment. The correlation of social background with achievement, illness, disability and many other aspects of life is as powerful now as it was when such relationships were studied by sociologists of education in the 1950s. Where catchment areas are relatively socially and economically homogeneous, schools serving different kinds of local communities are likely to find this reflected in their experience of special educational needs. It is also possible that classes within a school will vary in terms of their experience of special educational needs. This may arise from chance variations in intakes but could also reflect school policies with regard to meeting special educational needs.

The distribution of pupils with special needs across schools and classes is relevant to decisions about appropriate provision in two ways. First, there is the question of the extent to which special educational needs is an issue for all schools and all teachers, or whether it can be regarded as a specialist issue for those in areas where such needs are concentrated. Second, there is the question of the nature of the definition of special educational needs and the related question of the equitable distribution of resources. Some researchers have suggested that special educational needs, and especially learning difficulties, may be interpreted by schools in an entirely relativistic way. This would mean that the poorest-performing group of children relative to the rest of the school or class will be defined as having such needs whatever their absolute level of achievement. Resources could therefore be diverted away from the schools with the highest level of difficulty (Thomas and Davis, 1997).

In Table 3.3 the distribution of special educational needs across schools and classrooms is shown for both 1998 and 1981. Schools and classes have been grouped by the proportions of children in them described as having special educational needs. For example, the top row of the table shows that no school was without any pupils with special needs either in 1998 or 1981, but 3.5% of classes had no children with special needs in 1981, and 0.7% of classes had no children with special needs in 1998.

Table 3.3: Special educational needs 1981–98: variations across schools and classrooms

Proportions of pupils nominated as having special needs	Schools		Classes	
	1981 %	1998 %	1981 %	1998 %
0	0	0	3.5	0.7
>0–10%	21.3	2.2	18.0	9.5
>10%–20%	42.6	30.4	32.2	24.6
>20%–30%	29.5	30.4	26.8	30.2
>30%–40%	3.3	28.3	12.1	21.8
>40%–50%	3.3	4.3	5.8	6.7
>50%	0	4.3	1.4	6.7
N =	61	46	428	285

The distribution of schools in 1998 shows that it is not the case that children with special needs are concentrated in just a few schools. There were no schools where no child was described as having special needs and only 2.2% (that is, one school) where the proportion was 10% or less. At the other end of the scale, 4.3% (or two schools) regarded more than 50% of their pupils as having special needs. The data shows the very considerable range of special educational needs experienced by schools. However, it also shows a continuum of experience. The great majority of schools are in the three middle categories and there is no clear dividing line between schools which have and schools which do not have children with special educational needs. The comparison of the figures for 1998 with those for 1981 shows a broadly similar pattern of distribution. However, as we would expect from the figures discussed earlier, the distribution has shifted upwards. This shift corresponds very approximately to a shift upwards of one category of prevalence within the table.

The data for distribution of special educational needs across classrooms also shows both a considerable variation and also a very widespread prevalence of special needs. Only two teachers, 0.7% of the total, said that there were no pupils in their class on the Register of special needs. In all, just over 10% had 10% or fewer of their class on the Register. At the other extreme, 6.7% of teachers had more than half their class on the Register and a further 6.7% had between 40% and 50%. Most teachers, however, were in the central categories and had between 10% and 40% of their classes on the Register. Only one school had a policy of putting children with special educational needs together in a class, and the figures therefore include one class where all of the eight pupils were on the special needs Register. As with whole school figures, these results show a considerable variation in prevalence. Having 10% or fewer of the class (two or three children) on the Register of special educational needs clearly is a very different teaching situation than having 40% or higher, perhaps twelve or more pupils.

The results in Table 3.3 show the variation in prevalence of special needs, with some schools and teachers experiencing a very much higher level of such needs than others. In Chapter 4 we shall look at some of the factors associated with different levels of special educational needs. What is clear from the present analysis is that special educational needs are very widespread in the primary school system, but also that such needs are very much more prevalent in some contexts than others. It is clear that teachers are not simply regarding the lowest achieving children in their class as having special needs regardless of their overall level of achievement. The variation between schools and teachers is not compatible with an entirely relativistic interpretation of the concept of special needs. The question of whether the relation of children's achievements to those of other children in the class or school are relevant at all to their categorization as having special needs will be considered in the next chapter.

The comparison of the 1998 and 1981 figures shows that in both years special educational needs go across the school system and are an issue for all schools and all teachers. The changes over the seventeen years are in terms of a general upward movement in the prevalence of special needs. They do not indicate that special educational needs are becoming more concentrated, either into particular schools or, for the most part, into particular classes within schools.

STAGES OF THE SPECIAL NEEDS REGISTER

As we saw in Chapter 2 there have been considerable changes in the organization of provision for special educational needs in the past two decades and, in particular, a very considerable increase in the formalities of identification, assessment and record-keeping. A central feature of recent developments of this kind is the Register of special educational needs with its five-stage model for identifying and organizing provision for special needs. This is not a legal requirement on schools (although a great many teachers seem to believe that it is) but it was a universal practice in the schools in the study. A major difference between the 1998 survey and the earlier study was that it took place in the context of the Register. In 1981 teachers were asked in an initially open-ended fashion about all children currently in their class whom they regarded as having special educational needs. In 1998 teachers were asked about each Stage of the Register and the children who were on it. It was very unusual for a child who was not on the Register to be described by their teacher as having special educational needs.

The Register and its stages provides a structure for describing the severity of special educational needs and the extent of school and other provision to meet them. In Table 3.4 figures are presented for the proportions of children at each Stage. The first point to note is that virtually all the pupils regarded by their teachers as having special educational needs are on the Register. Only 1.5% of the children discussed were not on the Register and these were usually children new to the class and whom the teacher was expecting to be entered shortly.

The largest group of pupils, 10.5% of all children and 40.3% of those with special needs, were at Stage 1. This involves the initial expression of concern about a child and early action such as increased differentiation. A slightly smaller number of pupils was at Stage 2, 9.1% of all pupils and 35.0% of those with special needs. Stage 2 involves more intensive intervention and, in particular, an Individual Education Plan. Stage 3 is the point where outside specialists are involved: 4.2% of all pupils, 16% of those with special needs, were at Stage 3. Stages 1 to 3 are school-based Stages, although Stage 3 may

Table 3.4: Special educational needs 1998:
stages of the Register

	% of all pupils	% of CSEN
Not on Register	0.4	1.5
Stage 1	10.5	40.3
Stage 2	9.1	35.0
Stage 3	4.2	16.0
Stage 4	0.4	1.5
Stage 5	1.5	5.7
N =	8,149	2,123

involve considerable external input. Stages 4 and 5 are external to the school: Stage 4 is the point of statutory multi-professional assessment co-ordinated by the school psychological service and involving educational, medical and psychological input as well as parental involvement and, possibly, social service involvement. Stage 5 is reached when the assessment has resulted in a Statement of special educational needs. Many children with Statements are still educated in separate special schools but over half are now in mainstream education (Norwich, 1997). In 1998 at Key Stage 2 classrooms 0.4% of pupils were being assessed and 1.5% of pupils had Statements.

More than three-quarters of the children identified as having special educational needs are at the first two Stages of the process where they are firmly part of the ordinary responsibility of the school. Just under a quarter are at stages where they are thought to need help beyond that ordinarily available in school: this means about 6.1% of the mainstream school population. The external support these children need will range from some specialist advice to extensive external input. The largest group of children to whom this applies are at Stage 3 where the degree of external input is generally lower than for Stage 4 or 5 children. For some of those at Stage 5 a special school placement is a likely outcome as we shall see when the nature of the provision available to children at these Stages is considered in Chapter 6. But it is worth noting at this point that for 6.1% of the mainstream school population, that is, approaching an average of two children per class, some degree of support external to the school is felt to be necessary.

LEARNING DIFFICULTIES

As we have seen, difficulties with learning dominate teachers' perceptions of special educational needs in the Key Stage 2 classroom. This was also so in the 1981 survey but learning difficulties have increased in their predominance in the 1998 survey. The perceived prevalence of learning difficulties has increased considerably in 1998 compared with 1981 and to a much greater extent than other types of special educational need. This means that learning difficulties now make up an even higher proportion of special needs than in the earlier study. The 1981 survey provided fewer details of the nature of children's learning difficulties than did the present study. However, what did emerge from the earlier study was that most children with learning difficulties were seen as having 'all-round' or generalized learning difficulties rather than difficulties specific to particular aspects of their learning. But at the same time as the perception of children's difficulties as being non-specific, it was also apparent that, in practice, problems with reading were a very central aspect of teacher perceptions.

The 1998 study gathered details of the nature of children's learning difficulties, as perceived by their teachers, and these are presented in Table 3.5. As before, children's difficulties with learning are seen by their teachers as, for the most part, generalized or 'all-round' difficulties. Of all the children identified as having some sort of learning difficulty, 84.2%, about one in five of the total of children in the classrooms studied, were seen as having this sort of all-round difficulty with learning. In contrast, only 15.8% of those with learning difficulties, or about one in 25 of all children, had difficulties specific to one aspect of their learning.

Among the children with specific learning difficulties, by far the most common problem was a difficulty with reading. About 70% of all those children identified as having a specific learning difficulty had a problem with reading. More generally, language and literacy-related problems of some sort were the overwhelming aspect of specific difficulties as seen by the teachers. After problems with reading, problems with spelling and with writing were the most common aspects of specific learning difficulties. In contrast, only about 15% of those children with a specific learning difficulty had a problem with mathematics, one in 200 of all the children in the classrooms studied. As in the earlier study, the pattern to emerge is of a generally undifferentiated difficulty with learning dominating the perception of special educational needs, together with an emphasis on reading and

Table 3.5: Learning difficulties in 1998

	% of all pupils	% of learning difficulties
Generalized learning difficulty	19.5	84.2
(Dyslexia)	0.9	4.1
Specific learning difficulty	3.7	15.8
Reading	2.6	11.0
(Dyslexia)	(0.7)	(2.9)
Spelling	1.4	6.2
Writing	1.4	5.9
Mathematics	0.5	2.3
Speech and language	0.4	1.6
Under-achieving	0.1	0.4
Other	0.2	0.8
N =	8,149	1,884

related problems where difficulties are seen as more specific.

A particular aspect of problems with reading is the much-debated issue of dyslexia. For any child with reading difficulties the teacher was asked if these could be described as dyslexia. These results are given in two separate rows of Table 3.5, first for those children with generalized learning difficulties, and second for children with specific reading difficulties. Dyslexia is generally thought of as an aspect of specific reading difficulties and, in the present study, just over a quarter of the children with specific reading difficulties were described by their teachers as dyslexic. However, teachers also felt that some of the other children whose generalized learning difficulties included reading could be described as dyslexic. In absolute terms, more children with generalized learning difficulties were described as dyslexic than children with specific reading problems. Proportionately however, children with specific reading problems were much more likely to be described in this way.

EMOTIONAL AND BEHAVIOURAL PROBLEMS AND DISCIPLINE PROBLEMS

In the analysis of broad categories of special educational needs, children described as having emotional and behavioural difficulties and children described as being discipline problems were grouped together under a general 'emotional and behavioural' label. There was, of course, very considerable overlap between the categories of 'emotional and behavioural difficulty' and 'discipline problem', but also some children who only fell into one of the categories. From the data presented in Table 3.1 it was apparent that just under one in ten of the children in the classrooms studied had some sort of emotional, behavioural or discipline problem and that rather over half these children presented their teachers with discipline problems. More details of these figures are given in Table 3.6.

Table 3.6: Emotional and behavioural difficulties in 1998

	% of all pupils	% EBD and/or discipline
Emotional and behavioural difficulties and a discipline problem	4.3	46.8
Emotional and behavioural difficulties not a discipline problem	4.1	44.2
Discipline problem not an emotional and behavioural difficulty	0.8	9.0
N =	8,149	756

Table 3.6 shows that 4.3% of all children were described by their teachers as both having and emotional and behavioural difficulty and presenting a discipline problem. Almost the same proportion of children were described as having emotional and behavioural difficulties which did not present the teacher with discipline problems. This ratio was close to that to emerge from the 1981 survey. It shows that, then, as now, teachers do not equate emotional and behavioural difficulties with problems of classroom control and recognize such difficulties even when classroom discipline is not an issue. For a small proportion of pupils, under one in 100 overall and under one in ten of all those with emotional, behavioural or discipline problems, children were identified as presenting problems of classroom discipline but not as having any emotional and behavioural difficulty. These children were regarded by their teachers as 'naughty boys' (they were all boys), whose classroom behaviour gave the teacher problems, but was not an indicator of problems of personality or adjustment. The ratio of such children to all children regarded as presenting discipline problems was also very similar to that in 1981.

PHYSICAL DISABILITIES, SENSORY DIFFICULTIES AND HEALTH PROBLEMS

Unlike the other categories of special educational needs discussed here, the prevalence of physical, sensory and health-related problems has not increased since the 1981 survey. Further details of these difficulties are presented in Table 3.7 where figures are given separately for 'physical disability', 'health problems', 'visual difficulties' and 'hearing difficulties'. The severity of such difficulties varied considerably. There was a very small number of children in the classrooms who were blind or deaf, but some lesser degree of sight or hearing impairment was more common. Similarly, there were children in wheelchairs and with seriously disabling illnesses, but most children described in this way had less severe physical and health problems. It should be noted that these are areas in which teachers do not have a professional expertise, and some of their descriptions of children's problems explicitly revealed a degree of uncertainty about the difficulties they were describing.

Table 3.7: Physical, health and sensory difficulties in 1998

	% of all pupils	Proportion with learning difficulties
Physical disability	1.3	.84
Health problems	1.9	.83
Visual difficulty	1.4	.86
Hearing difficulty	1.1	.87
N =	8,149	

It was noted in the discussion of Table 3.2 that a high proportion of children with physical, health and sensory difficulties also had learning difficulties. Table 3.7 shows that this is virtually constant across the different types of difficulty: children with physical, health, hearing and sight problems are all very likely to have learning difficulties; about four times as likely as children without such problems. A comparison with the figures from the 1981 survey shows that the extent to which children with physical, sensory and health problems also have learning difficulties has increased since the earlier study from a proportion of 0.64 to 0.85. However, this should be put in the context of the overall increase in the proportion of children seen as having learning difficulties over this period. The increase in the proportion of children with physical health and sensory difficulties also experiencing learning difficulties is no greater than the increase in learning difficulties among children generally.

SUMMARY

The prevalence of special educational needs overall, and of different kinds, and the comparison between the 1998 figures and those from 1981 provide the core of the data to emerge from this study. In summary, just over a quarter of all children in mainstream Key Stage 2 classrooms were on the Register of special educational needs in 1998, a very considerable increase compared with the already substantial figure from 1981. The great majority of these children, almost 90%, had difficulties with learning, and difficulties of this kind showed the greatest degree of increase since the earlier study. Emotional and behavioural difficulties, including discipline problems, had also increased, but not to the same extent as learning difficulties. Health, sensory and physical difficulties had remained at the same level as in 1981. As before, there was a considerable degree of overlap between these categories and many children had more than one type of special educational need. Schools and classrooms showed considerable variation in the proportion of pupils having special educational needs. Nevertheless, as in the earlier study, it was clear that such needs were very widespread through the educational system and are issues for all schools and all teachers.

Child and school factors related to special educational needs

In the previous chapter we described the extent of special educational needs as seen by teachers and schools. In this discussion we dealt with the overall pattern of special needs and different categories of special needs, but did not relate these to other characteristics of children. The present chapter will extend our understanding of special educational needs in mainstream primary schools by looking at the relationship of special educational needs to other sorts of information about children and their schools.

In particular, we shall be concerned with the different patterns of special educational needs occurring between boys and girls, different patterns among different ethnic groups, the prevalence of special needs among different year groups in the Key Stage 2 age range, and the relationship between special educational needs and indicators of poverty. We shall also be looking at the relationship between special educational needs and measures of educational achievement, both overall and in the context of the levels of achievement in the school in which children are located. Wherever possible this analysis will be related to data from the 1981 survey.

The analysis presented here has two inter-related aspects. The first is to describe the nature and severity of some of the difficulties, especially difficulties in learning, experienced by children with special educational needs, and to see if these difficulties are experienced differentially between different groups of children. The second aspect is to explore the extent to which characteristics of children such as age, gender or ethnicity, or characteristics of schools and classes, such as poverty and overall levels of performance, may influence the judgement teachers make of whether individual pupils have special educational needs.

In the 1981 survey systematic patterns of difference were found between different groups of children. The most striking difference was that between boys and girls: boys in the classrooms studied were almost twice as likely as girls to be regarded by their teachers as having special educational needs. Differences related to ethnicity were also found: pupils from ethnic minority backgrounds were about a third more likely than white children to be regarded as having special educational needs. There were also age differences: a higher proportion of the youngest age group (7 to 8 year olds) were categorized as having special educational needs than those in the oldest age group (10 to 11 year olds).

In considering differences between groups of children of this kind there are two sets of tensions of which we need to be aware. The first has already been mentioned above: the extent to which these differences reflect differences in characteristics of children which are part of their learning, behaviour or health, compared with the extent to which they reflect other characteristics of children which in some way influence teacher perceptions of such things. We can explore this further, particularly in relation to learning difficulties, when we consider the relationship of special educational needs to reading assessments and other measures of attainment.

The second tension is to do with the consequences for children of being identified as having special educational needs. This is the dilemma for teachers and schools, noted, for example, by Norwich (1993). It is necessary to assess and identify children if schools are to respond to their needs appropriately. But, at the same time, such assessment and identification marks children as different in a potentially negative fashion. If certain groups of children are over-represented among those identified as having special educational needs, it is not necessarily clear whether such groups are advantaged by being given additional access to resources or whether they may be disadvantaged by being picked out as different and, in some way, problematic. This is an enduring tension in special educational needs and in education more generally. However, we shall try to address it to some extent when we consider the provision made available to children with different sorts of difficulties in Chapter 6.

GENDER, ETHNICITY, AGE AND SPECIAL EDUCATIONAL NEEDS

In Tables 4.1, 4.2 and 4.3, the proportions of children in different groups are compared with regard to the prevalence of special educational needs. Comparisons with the 1981 figures are also given. Table 4.1 shows the comparison of boys and girls for the two years. The over-representation of boys among children experiencing difficulties in school is a very well-established phenomenon. Recent concern has focused on an apparent increase in such difficulties and, in particular, on the issue of boys' 'underachievement'. The figures in Table 4.1 confirm the preponderance of boys among children with special educational needs but do not support the argument that this is an increasing problem. In 1981 boys outnumbered girls among children with special educational needs by a ratio of just under two to one. In 1998 they also outnumber girls and the proportions of both boys and girls with special educational needs has increased. However, the ratio of boys to girls is slightly lower in 1998 than it was in 1981 (1.65:1 compared with 1.85:1). The relative increase in the proportions of girls with special educational needs has been greater: although, of course, a greater number of additional boys than girls are now included in this category.

Table 4.1: Gender and special educational needs: 1998 and 1981

	1998		1981	
	Male %	Female %	Male %	Female %
Any special educational needs	32.1	19.5	24.4	13.2
Learning difficulties	27.7	18.1	19.5	11.1
Emotional and behavioural difficulties	14.3	4.0	10.9	4.5
(Discipline problems)*	(8.7)	(1.5)	(6.4)	(1.7)
Physical, sensory and health problems	5.6	2.9	5.8	2.9
N =	4,156	3,993	6,275	6,035
	(51.0)	(49.0)	(51.0)	(49.0)

* Also included in 'emotional and behavioural difficulties'

The area where the difference between boys and girls has increased is that of emotional and behavioural difficulties. The proportion of girls regarded by their teachers as having emotional and behavioural difficulties has decreased slightly between 1981 and 1998. Even more strikingly, the proportion of girls regarded as presenting their teachers with discipline problems has decreased over the period. The increase in the proportion of children regarded as having emotional and behavioural difficulties is almost entirely a male phenomenon, and the disparity between boys and girls has widened further, especially in the case of discipline problems.

Table 4.2: Ethnicity and special educational needs: 1998 and 1981

	1998			1981		
	All ethnic minorities %	White %	Afro-Caribbean %	All ethnic minorities %	White %	Afro-Caribbean %
Any special educational needs	22.2	26.3	27.0	24.1	18.0	24.2
Learning difficulties	19.7	23.5	20.5	21.1	14.6	18.4
Emotional and behavioural difficulties (Discipline problems)	9.0 (5.5)	9.3 (5.1)	14.2 (7.4)	7.3 (4.5)	7.8 (4.0)	16.6 (14.1)
Physical, sensory and health problems	4.0	4.3	6.4	4.6	4.5	5.1
N =	1,255 (15.4)	6,894 (84.6)	204 (2.5)	1,282 (10.4)	11,004 (89.6)	277 (2.3)

In Table 4.2 the results are given from a comparison of different ethnic groups over time with respect to different sorts of special educational needs. The question of ethnicity and both educational achievement and special educational needs more generally is both complex and sensitive. The present study was not principally designed to investigate ethnic differences, and the results presented here must be treated cautiously. When teachers were describing children in their classes with special educational needs they were asked about the ethnic group to which each child belonged. In the interviews with headteachers each head was asked about the proportion of children in the school belonging to different ethnic groups. In principle this allows us to calculate the proportions of children in different ethnic groups nominated by their teachers as having different sorts of special educational needs. There are, however, various difficulties with such a procedure. Questions of ethnicity are both complex and contested. Both teachers and headteachers used some fairly general terminology ('Asian', 'mixed-race') and were in some cases unsure of the ethnic origin of their pupils. Recent work on ethnicity and educational achievement has shown the very considerable diversity in the educational achievements of children from different ethnic minority groups (Gillborn and Gipps, 1996). In the present analysis we have therefore used a dichotomy between 'white' and 'ethnic minority' pupils, accepting that a wide variety of different types of origin are incorporated in both categories. Additionally we have also used the category 'Afro-Caribbean'. This is used both because it was a group in which teachers and headteachers were generally unambiguous in their identifications, and also because this group of pupils has been of particular concern, both with regard to educational achievement and with regard to racism within the educational system. Pupils categorized as 'Afro-Caribbean' in Table 4.2 are also included in the data for ethnic minority pupils generally. This type of analysis also facilitates a comparison with the 1981 data. The very imprecise category 'Asian' used in 1981 has been combined with the category 'West Indian', used at that time to provide a comparison with the 1998 'ethnic minority' category. The figures for 'West Indians' in 1981 has been re-named 'Afro-Caribbean' for comparison with the 1998 figures.

In 1981, children from ethnic minorities were over-represented by about a third in the children regarded as having special educational needs. Within the overall ethnic minority category there was no difference between children of Afro-Caribbean origin and other ethnic minorities. The main reason for the over-representation of children from ethnic minority backgrounds was their over-representation among children with learning difficulties. Analysis of the 1981 data showed that a substantial proportion of such difficulties was related to the language problems of children of South Asian or East African-Asian origin whose families had recently emigrated to the United Kingdom. Ethnic minority children generally were not over-represented among children with emotional and behavioural difficulties or children with health, sensory or physical difficulties. The sub-group of children of Afro-Caribbean origin, about a quarter of the children from ethnic minorities, was less likely than other ethnic minority children to be seen as having learning difficulties, although they were more likely than white children to have such difficulties. However, children of Afro-Caribbean origin were more than twice as likely as other children, either white or other ethnic minority, to be regarded as having emotional and behavioural difficulties. Even more strikingly, they were more than three times as likely as other children to present their teachers with discipline problems. While drawing attention to these substantial differences, the report on the 1981 survey also made the important point that they still related to a fairly small proportion of children overall: the great majority of children, of whatever ethnic group, were not regarded as having special educational needs and did not present their teachers with problems in the classroom.

The figures in Table 4.2 provide a comparison between the 1981 figures and the situation in 1998. The first point to emerge is that, unlike the earlier figures, children from ethnic minorities are no longer over-represented among children with special educational needs. The proportion of ethnic minority children is now lower than that for white children and, unlike white children, there has been a decrease in the proportion of children with special educational needs in 1998 compared with 1981.

A more detailed look at the different categories of special educational need shows where these differences have occurred. The proportion of children from ethnic minorites with health, sensory or physical difficulties has declined very slightly, as has that for children more generally. The proportion of children from ethnic minority backgrounds with emotional and behavioural difficulties has increased somewhat, to about the same extent as that for white pupils. The figures for ethnic minority and white pupils are very similar with regard to both emotional and behavioural difficulties and discipline problems in 1981 and 1998. Where the difference has occurred is in respect of learning difficulties. In the overall context of a substantial increase in the proportions of children regarded as having learning difficulties, the proportion of children from ethnic minorities having such difficulties has shown a decrease. This result supports the argument, put forward in the report on the 1981 study, that the over-representation of children from ethnic minorities was largely the result of very specific factors connected with language difficulties: these included recent migration, and English not being the language of the home. Such issues are much less prevalent in the 1998 survey.

Of course, the figures in Table 4.2 and the discussion above inevitably represents an over-simplification of complex patterns of educational experience and, in particular, combines the educational experiences of pupils from very different ethnic backgrounds. One group for which it is possible to provide a more precise analysis is children of Afro-Caribbean origin. In 1981 these pupils were as likely to be regarded as having special educational needs as other ethnic minority pupils, and more likely than white pupils. They were very much more likely than other pupils to be regarded as having emotional and behavioural difficulties and to present teachers with discipline problems. As Table 4.2 shows, the pattern of change over time for children of Afro-Caribbean origin differs both from that of other ethnic minority pupils and from white pupils. Unlike the aggregated figure for all ethnic minority groups, the proportion of children of Afro-Caribbean origin described as having special educational needs has not decreased. However, nor has it shown the major increase that the figures for white pupils show. The proportionate increase for the Afro-Caribbean group has been much less than for white children, or for children in general, and there was in 1998 very little difference in the proportion of white and Afro-Caribbean children described as having special educational needs.

This different trajectory of change is also apparent in the more detailed analysis of different categories of special educational needs. The proportion of children of Afro-Caribbean origin regarded as having learning difficulties has only shown a small increase compared with that for children more generally. In comparison with 1981, in 1998 these children were less likely than white children to be described as having learning difficulties. The difference in patterns of change is even more striking in the case of emotional and behavioural difficulties. As in 1981, in 1998 children from Afro-Caribbean backgrounds were more likely than any other group to be described both as having emotional and behavioural difficulties and as presenting discipline problems in the classroom. However, unlike every other group, this proportion has declined between the two surveys. Children from Afro-Caribbean backgrounds are rather less likely to be described as having emotional and behavioural difficulties and are half as likely to be described as presenting discipline problems in 1998 compared with 1981. As the proportion of other children in these categories has increased, the gap between Afro-Caribbean children and other children has narrowed considerably. This result is particularly dramatic in the case of discipline problems.

These results lend support to some of the concerns about the educational experiences of ethnic minority pupils and, especially, the educational experiences of pupils from Afro-Caribbean backgrounds. However, they also present a more positive picture than some other recent evidence and a more positive picture than the 1981 survey. As a group, ethnic minority pupils are not more likely than white pupils to be regarded by their teachers as having special educational needs, and the proportion having such needs has decreased in the period between the two surveys. Of course this overall result disguises many variations within the overall category 'ethnic minority'. Children from Afro-Caribbean backgrounds, who have been the focus of considerable concern, are only slightly more likely than white children to be regarded as having special educational needs and are less likely to be regarded as having learning difficulties. Worryingly, they are still more likely than any other group to be regarded as having emotional and behavioural difficulties and to present their teachers with discipline problems. However, the disparity between this group and other children is very much less than in 1981, and the Afro-Caribbean pupils are the only group where teachers' perceptions of this sort of difficulty has decreased over time.

A third factor, after gender and ethnicity, to be considered here is that of the year group of pupils within the Key Stage 2 age range. In 1981 there was a small but fairly consistent tendency for the level of special educational needs to reduce as pupils moved through what was then the junior school age phase. More of the younger children than older children were identified by their teachers and, although the differences were not great, there was a consistent decrease across the four years of junior schooling. The only exception to this pattern was, perhaps not surprisingly, discipline problems where the prevalence increased as children got older. In the earlier study it was suggested that this pattern reflected both real changes in children over time and also changes in teacher perceptions. If some of the earlier problems reflected immaturity and late development on the part of children it is likely that these will become less prevalent as children get older and therefore that the incidence of difficulties will decrease. However, it was also suggested that teacher perceptions of children's relative degrees of difficulty may be different for younger and older children. A 7-year-old pupil who is rather behind her or his age peers may be struggling on the verge of literacy, while an 11 year old in the same relative position may nevertheless be coping in class. Consequently, teachers may be more inclined to describe younger children as having special educational needs.

The 1998 data makes it possible to see if the age differences noted in the 1981 study still occurred. It was initially hypothesized that the increased formality and regulation of the assessment and registration of children as having special educational needs may have reduced the age differences found in the earlier study, and produced a more consistent pattern of incidence of special educational needs across year groups. However, it was also noted during the interviews with teachers and special educational needs co-ordinators that children in Year 3, the first year of Key Stage 2, sometimes seemed to be on the Register of special educational needs as a precaution, rather than because the school had clearly identified problems they were experiencing. This was especially so in schools which only catered for Key Stage 2 children and had feeder infant schools (Key Stage 1). In these schools children sometimes arrived from the feeder school already on the Register of special educational needs and were kept there for the year, even though the school could not really identify a special educational need.

Table 4.3 is based on those children in single age-group classes and ignores the possible complications which may arise in assessing special educational needs when children are in mixed age classes. The figures in the table show the pattern across age groups and allow the possible influences of the factors outlined above to be evaluated. It is clear that the consistent pattern of decreasing prevalence of special educational needs as children get older, which was apparent in 1981, was not occurring in 1998. The level of special educational needs remained virtually constant across Years 3, 4 and 5. It is only at Year 6, the final year of primary schooling, that the drop in prevalence with increased age, which was evident in the earlier study, appears. Apart from the decrease in Year 6 it is hard to see a consistent pattern across the year groups. There is a slight peak in Year 5, especially in the case of learning difficulties and, as in the earlier survey (against the 1981 trend), there is an increase in discipline problems as children get older through Years 3, 4 and 5. Even here there is a decrease at Year 6. The figures do not support the suggestions to emerge from the interviews that schools may be putting Year 3 children onto the special needs Register on a 'safety first' basis, especially when this group of pupils is new to the school. However, they also do not clearly support the position that more formalized procedures lead to a more uniform pattern of assessment across the different year groups. Prevalence is much more consistent across Years 3, 4 and 5 in 1998 compared with 1981. However, the decrease in prevalence with age, which was a fairly smooth trend in 1981, re-occurs in Year 6 in the later study.

PUPIL ATTAINMENT AND SPECIAL EDUCATIONAL NEEDS

The discussion so far has focused on the occurrence of special educational needs as defined by teachers in the mainstream primary schools in the survey. The issue of definition and the relationship between the difficulties children experience at school, the provision that schools make for them and the notion of 'special' applied to children's educational needs has already been considered in Chapter 2. These difficulties and, in particular, the circularity in the relationship between extra provision and the specialness of needs will be returned to when we consider the kind of provision offered to children on the Register of special educational needs. At this point we shall attempt to better understand the way in which 'special' is applied by teachers

Table 4.3: Year group and special educational needs: 1998 and 1981

	1998				1981			
	Year 3 %	Year 4 %	Year 5 %	Year 6 %	Year 3 %	Year 4 %	Year 5 %	Year 6 %
Any special educational needs	26.1	25.3	27.2	21.5	21.1	19.5	18.3	16.4
Learning difficulties	22.6	21.7	24.5	19.5	17.8	16.1	14.7	13.2
Emotional and behavioural difficulties (Discipline problems)	8.1 (4.0)	9.5 (5.5)	10.6 (6.2)	7.9 (4.1)	8.2 (3.7)	7.6 (3.9)	7.9 (4.3)	7.2 (4.3)
Physical, sensory and health problems	4.0	5.5	5.0	4.0	5.5	4.6	3.7	3.9
N =	1,500	1,338	1,341	1,402	2,832	3,001	3,234	3,243

and schools by looking at the available measures of academic attainment available for children nominated in the survey.

The great majority of schools in the study keep measures of reading achievement, usually in the forms of reading ages, for all pupils. These are the only measures which are kept uniformly enough to be of use in comparisons between different schools and different children. (National Curriculum assessments would only be available for a minority of children in the full Key Stage 2 age range, and are in any case much too crude at an individual level to be used for this purpose.) It must be remembered that these measures come from a variety of different tests, administered in different circumstances by the schools and not the research team: the results must therefore be treated cautiously. However, they are all based on standardized measures of reading achievement, intended to be administered by teachers and designed both to monitor overall levels of achievement and as indicators of reading difficulties. As we saw in Chapter 3, in both the surveys, reading performance was the major aspect of concern over children's learning.

Table 4.4 compares the reading achievements, as measured by school-administered reading tests, of children described by their teachers as having any kind of learning difficulty in 1981 and in 1998. In 1981 the median reading age of children with learning difficulties was one year and eight months behind their chronological age. Just under half of these children (45.8%) were two years or more behind and a further 30% were at least a year behind. A quarter of the children described as having learning difficulties had reading ages of less than one year or more behind. (A few of these children were not behind in reading at all, although figures for this were not calculated in the earlier study.)

In 1998 the median gap between reading age and chronological age of children described as having learning difficulties was one year and nine months. About 42% of these children were at least a year behind, a slightly lower figure than in 1981. A further 38% were at least a year behind, rather higher than the equivalent figure for 1981, and 20% were less than a year behind, fewer than in 1981. Of the 20% of children with learning difficulties with reading ages less than a year behind their chronological ages, 6% were not behind at all.

Table 4.4: Reading ages of pupils with learning difficulties: 1998 and 1981

	1998	1981
RA two years or more behind CA	41.9%	44.8%
RA one year behind but less than two years behind CA	38.0%	30.2%
RA less than one year behind CA	14.2%	25.0%
RA not behind CA	6.0%	
Median difference between CA and RA	−1 year 9 months	−1 year 8 months
N =	1,455	1,405

The children included in the figures in Table 4.4 have to meet two criteria: they must be in the various reading age categories and they must also be identified by their school and teacher as having learning difficulties. The interplay of these two factors means that interpretation of the results must be cautious. However, it is clear from the table that children identified as having learning difficulties in 1998 had a very slightly lower median reading age compared with those identified in 1981. As we have seen, the proportion of children described by their teachers as having learning difficulties increased by 50% between the two surveys. The reading-age figures show that this cannot be because of a systematic tendency to identify learning difficulties at a lesser level of severity than in the earlier year. It is not the case that children whose levels of reading achievement were not regarded as constituting a special educational need in 1981 were, in general, so regarded in 1998.

The figures on the gap between reading age and chronological age in Table 4.4 allow this finding to be explored further. In 1998, compared with the earlier figures, a lower proportion of the children described as having learning difficulties are in the extreme categories: either two years or more behind or less than a year behind. A higher proportion were in the central category of between one and two years behind. In the analysis of the original survey it was suggested that a gap between reading age and chronological age of about two years was something of a watershed in teacher perceptions of such difficulties. Children who were that far behind were fairly consistently described by their teachers as having learning and reading problems. In this case the assessment was fairly independent of other characteristics of the children or the overall levels of achievement of the classes and schools in which they were taught. On the other hand, children who were less than two years behind were assessed as having special educational needs in a less consistent fashion Other factors such as overall levels of class achievement, as well as more idiosyncratic influences, came to bear.

Extending this discussion to a comparison with the 1998 figures suggests that the results are compatible with there being no substantial change in the levels of difficulty experienced by children between the two surveys; and, at the same time, an increase in consistency of assessment and also in the extent to which teachers identify such difficulties, especially when they are less severe. The decreasing proportion of children who are two years or more behind suggests that there has not been an overall shift downwards in levels of achievement. The increase in the proportion of children between one and two years behind and the decrease in the proportion less than one year behind is consistent with a more uniform pattern of assessment.

The levels of reading achievement of pupils nominated by their teachers as having learning difficulties can also be used to compare different groups of children. As with the earlier analysis it is important to remember that these are children described by their teachers as having learning difficulties, and the figures do not describe differences between different groups of children more generally. In Table 4.5 the median gap between reading age and chronological age is presented for boys and girls, different ethnic groups and the different year groups within Key Stage 2. (As before, children from Afro-Caribbean backgrounds are listed separately but are also included in the 'ethnic minority' figures.)

Table 4.5: Reading achievement and learning difficulties: gender, ethnicity and year group, 1998

		Median Gap between Reading Age and Chronological Age	
		RA–CA	N
Gender	Male	−1 year 9 months	891
	Female	−1 year 7 months	558
Ethnicity	Ethnic minority	−1 year 10 months	162
	White	−1 year 9 months	1,282
	Afro-Caribbean	−1 year 7 months	36
Year Group	Year 3	−1 year 5 months	383
	Year 4	−1 year 9 months	358
	Year 5	−2 years 0 months	354
	Year 6	−2 years 3 months	316

The figures for boys and girls in Table 4.5 show that girls described by their teachers as having learning difficulties have slightly higher reading scores than boys described in this way. The median gap between reading age and chronological age is two months less for girls than for boys. This comparison shows that the considerable over-representation of boys among children with special educational needs has not come about as a result of boys being 'over-identified', at least in comparison with their overall levels of achievement: the learning difficulties of the boys in this group, at least as measured by reading ages, are slightly more severe than those of the girls.

The figures for different ethnic groups also show patterns of difference in the gap between reading age and chronological age. White children have the same gap as that of the children in the survey overall, as would be expected from their numerical predominance. Children from ethnic minority backgrounds generally have a median reading age one month further behind their chronological age than other children. This suggests that such children may be slightly 'under-identified', although the difference is very small. However, as a sub-set of the ethnic minority category, children from Afro-Caribbean backgrounds have a gap of two months less than that for 'white' children and three months less than for the overall ethnic minority group. This result also matches the analysis in the report of the 1981 survey. There it was suggested that there may be a tendency for teachers to over-identify Afro-Caribbean children as being what were then described as 'slow learners'.

Taken together, these results show that the over-representation of boys among children with learning difficulties does not come about because of a tendency for teachers to be more ready to identify them in this way at particular levels of achievement. However, the figures also show that the under-representation of ethnic minority pupils may reflect a slight tendency for teachers to under-identify them. This is not the case for children from Afro-Caribbean backgrounds, where a small under-representation among children with learning difficulties is accompanied by evidence of a slight tendency to over-identify these children at particular levels of reading difficulty.

The situation with regard to the relationship between reading achievement and identification as having learning difficulties across different year groups, also presented in Table 4.5, is rather different from that for gender and ethnic groups. Differences here are likely to reflect different perceptions of the severity of different types of learning difficulty related to children's development, and possibly also to the assessment of reading performance at different ages. The pattern to emerge in Table 4.5 is predictable and is similar to that in 1981. Children identified as having learning difficulties in the early years of schooling have a much smaller gap between their reading age and chronological age than do children identified in the later years. The difference is between one year and five months for the Year 3 children (7/8 year olds) and two years and three months for the Year 6 children (10/11 year olds). This is a consistent tendency across the four years of Key Stage 2 and differs from the pattern of changing prevalence across these years to emerge from Table 4.3. The increasing severity of the reading problems of identified children is not reflected in a decreasing proportion of such children until Year 6. In Year 6, although the proportion of children described by their teachers as having learning difficulties has decreased somewhat, these children have fairly serious difficulties in that, on average, they are well over two years behind their age norm.

SCHOOL FACTORS AND SPECIAL EDUCATIONAL NEEDS

The purpose of many of the Government initiatives in special educational needs, as with many initiatives in other areas, was to ensure greater uniformity and consistency in practice across different schools and local education authorities. At the same time, the identification of special educational needs and the provision made for them takes place within specific educational contexts, and such contexts may be important in understanding how these educational decisions are made. This is especially likely to be the case given the potential circularity in the definition of special educational needs and provision made for it that were discussed in Chapter 2. It is also important to be aware of the extent to which schools differ with regard to the socio-economic composition of the areas they serve, and the likely impact of such differences on the prevalence of special educational needs.

In the remainder of this chapter we shall consider the characteristics of schools in the study using the proportion of children taking free school meals as an indicator of socio-economic disadvantage and the proportion of Year 6 children achieving Level 4 in the 1997 National Curriculum Assessments as an indicator of overall levels of achievement. We shall consider the variation between schools in these indicators, their relationship to the prevalence of special educational needs in the schools and whether schools with different overall levels of achievement differ with regard to the achievements of children identified as having learning difficulties. It should be noted that some of the analysis below deals with variables measured at school level rather than at individual level. It is therefore concerned to describe relationships between various characteristics of schools rather than of individual pupils. Relevant discussions are in Gibson and Asthana (1998) and Taylor Fitz-Gibbon (1996).

Detailed information on children with special educational needs is available from 46 schools; for 40 of these 1997 SAT scores are also available. (Two schools were in areas where children transfer from primary school at age 10, three schools had fewer Year 6 children take the SATs than results are reported for, and one school had re-opened after re-organization.) Data on the proportion of children receiving free school meals were available from 44 schools.

Schools in the survey varied widely both with regard to overall achievement and with regard to free school meals. The average percentage of children gaining Level 4 at the end of Key Stage 2 (averaged across English, Mathematics and Science) was 57.2, slightly below the average across the country. In the highest performing school almost 95% of children reached this level. In contrast, in the least well-performing school only one child in five averaged Level 4 across the three SAT areas. Such differences are clearly of considerable potential relevance for the prevalence of special educational needs in schools. The average proportion of children receiving free school meals was 28.9%, rather higher than the average for primary schools across the country. The school with the highest level of deprivation by this measure had two-thirds of its pupils receiving free school meals. At the other end of the scale was a school with just 2% of pupils receiving free school meals. The relationship between poverty and free school meals at school (not individual) level will be considered both in terms of an impact mediated by overall levels of achievement and direct impact.

The widely established relationship between socio-economic circumstances and academic achievement was repeated in the present study. The correlation between the proportion of children receiving free school meals and the proportion of children at Level 4 or above on the SATs was –0.73 One way of interpreting this is that well over a half of the variation between schools in their SAT outcomes could be accounted for by variations in the levels of poverty in the communities they serve. It is important to note that this is a school-level analysis and does not establish a correlation at individual level between poverty and academic achievement (although there is, of course, other evidence of this). It does show that the socio-economic circumstances of a school are highly predictive of its levels of achievement.

The relationship between these measures and special educational needs are presented in Table 4.6 where correlation coefficients describing the relationship between SAT scores and free school meals and different types of special educational needs and different stages of the Register of special educational need are given. The table shows a strong correlation between the overall level of special educational needs in a school and overall levels of achievement, and also a strong correlation between most categories of special need and overall achievement. Not only learning difficulties but also emotional and behavioural difficulties are correlated with overall levels of performance. The only exception is the prevalence of health, sensory and physical difficulties where there is no association with performance. One important conclusion from this result is that it shows that schools and teachers are not using the concept of special educational need and, in particular, the concept of learning difficulty, in a merely relativistic fashion. If teachers were interpreting the idea of special need just by reference to their own pupils and identifying the weakest whatever their absolute levels of achievement, then the correlations would be close to zero. The strong negative correlations show that schools where overall levels of achievement are low identify a much higher proportion of their pupils as having special educational needs than do schools where overall levels of achievement are high.

The correlations between the proportion of children receiving free school meals and the various types of special need show a similar pattern to that for the achievement measures, but of a generally weaker nature. Special needs generally and, more specifically, learning difficulties and emotional and behavioural difficulties all

Table 4.6: School level correlation between achievement, deprivation and special educational needs

	1997 SATs	1998 free school meals	1998 FSM controlling for SATs
All special educational needs	−0.55	0.34	−0.11
Learning difficulties	−0.53	0.34	−0.08
Emotional and behavioural difficulties (Discipline problems)	−0.56 (−0.63)	0.48 (0.69)	0.13 (0.44)
Health, sensory and physical difficulties	−0.08	0.09	0.05

Stages of the SEN
Register and 1997 SATS

Stage 1	−0.23
Stage 2	−0.49
Stage 3	−0.48
Stage 4	−0.12
Stage 5	0.18

correlate positively with free school meals: the higher the proportion of children receiving free school meals, the higher the proportion in each of these categories of special need. As with the SAT scores, the exception to this pattern is the prevalence of health, sensory and physical difficulties where there is no correlation with free school meals. The free school meals correlations are generally weaker than those with SAT scores. The one exception to this is the extent to which children are seen as discipline problems. The negative correlation of this measure with overall performance is high, but the correlation of the prevalence of discipline problems with free school meals is even higher.

The third column of Table 4.6 presents the partial correlations of free school meals with the special needs measures, controlling for SAT scores. As we have seen, there is a very strong correlation (−0.73) between the overall level of achievement in schools, as measured by SAT scores, and the extent of social deprivation measured by the extent of free school meals. Both SAT scores and free school meals correlate strongly with most of the measures of special educational needs. The question therefore arises of whether these associations are independent of one another or whether the relationship of one of the variables to special educational needs is explained or mediated by another. Clearly, in any causal relationship between deprivation and achievement, deprivation will be the prior variable. We therefore need to test the possibilities that:

(a) deprivation influences both overall achievement and special educational needs and influences each independently of its influence on the other; and

(b) that the relationship between deprivation and special educational needs is mediated by the influence of deprivation on achievement.

The first order partial correlations in Table 4.6 shows the relationship between free school meals and the special needs measures after the relationship of both with SAT scores has been accounted for. If the correlations are similar to the original correlations this would indicate that the relationship of free school meals and special needs was independent of the relationship of free school meals and achievement. If the correlations reduce to close to zero this would indicate that the relationship between free school meals and special needs is entirely mediated by the influence of overall achievement.

In general, the figures in column 3 of the table support the latter explanation. Most of the correlations between free school meals and special educational needs reduce to close to zero when SAT results are controlled. This is not only true of learning difficulties but is also true of special educational needs overall and also emotional and behavioural difficulties. (It should, of course, be remembered that almost nine out of ten children with special educational needs have learning difficulties, and that more than three-quarters of the children with emotional and behavioural difficulties had learning difficulties.) In general then, deprivation is strongly negatively related to overall school performance, and overall school performance is strongly negatively related to the prevalence of special educational needs. For most aspects of special educational needs, the link with deprivation is entirely, or virtually entirely, mediated by overall levels of school achievement.

The exception to this pattern is the extent of discipline problems in the schools in the study. As the figures in the first two columns of Table 4.6 show, the prevalence of discipline problems is strongly correlated with both SAT scores and with free school meals. Unlike the other associations however, the correlation between the prevalence of discipline problems and free school meals does not disappear when SAT scores are controlled. The correlation is reduced but is still very substantial. These figures show that there is an association between deprivation and discipline problems in schools, which is partly mediated by overall levels of achievement but mainly operates independently of achievement levels.

Table 4.6 also presents the correlations between school SAT scores and the proportions of children in the school at different stages of the Register of special educational needs. The high overall negative correlation between achievement levels and the proportion of pupils on the Register disguises different patterns across different Stages. The correlation between Stages 2 and 3 and the SAT scores reflects the overall correlation. At these Stages, where the pupils have Individual Education Plans, the association with achievement levels is at its strongest. At Stages 4 and 5 (that small proportion of children with the most severe level of difficulties likely to be experienced in mainstream schools), there is no association between the proportion of children and achievement levels. At Stage 1 (the level where children have been identified and are being monitored, but are not usually additionally resourced and may not have any different pedagogic or curricula provision), there is an association with achievement levels but one that is very much weaker than that for Stages 2 and 3. While overall achievement levels are very predictive of the difficulties that result in children being at Stage 2 or 3 of the Register, they are not at all predictive of the much more infrequent and serious difficulties that lead to children being at Stages 4 and 5. These difficulties appear to be less a part of the continuum of learning and related problems than are the difficulties at lower Stages, and less predictable in their occurrence.

The weaker correlation at Stage 1 suggests that a different process may be operating as, in principle, it might have been expected that overall achievement levels would have been at least as good a predictor as for Stages 2 and 3. It seems that there is more variation in practice across schools at the first stage of the Register than would be expected from other measures of the difficulties their pupils face. It suggests that practices in placing children at Stage 1 of the Register may vary between schools to a greater extent than at other Stages. This view is congruent with comments made by some class teachers during the interviews, which suggest a degree of uncertainty about the purpose of Stage 1 and the criteria for children being on it.

The data presented in Table 4.7 give a sense of what the correlations in Table 4.6 mean in terms of the proportions of children with special educational needs in different types of school. The 40 schools for which SAT data are available have been grouped into four categories, from those with the lowest level of overall achievement to those with the highest. The boundaries of the categories were arrived at using the two criteria of aiming for fairly evenly sized groups and looking for 'natural breaks' in the distribution of SAT scores.

As we would expect from the correlations there is a consistent trend across the four categories. In the lowest-achieving eight schools, 37.1% of pupils are described as having special educational needs, while in the highest-achieving ten schools this figure is 20.5%. The results show that schools differ very considerably in their experience of special needs, with lower-achieving schools having almost double the level of such needs as higher-achieving schools. However, they also show that special needs are widespread throughout the school system and that even schools with high levels of overall attainment still have about one in five of their pupils on the special educational needs Register.

Table 4.7: Special educational needs and school achievement levels

| | School SAT score | | | |
	20–35	>35–60	>60–75	>75
% pupils with SEN	37.1	27.2	24.5	20.5
N of schools	8	14	8	10
Median RA-CA of pupils with learning difficulties	−2 years 1 month	−1 year 10 months	−1 year 5 months	−1 year 6 months
N of pupils	305	691	185	225

The levels of difficulty experienced by children with learning difficulties in different types of school can be seen in the lower half of Table 4.7. The median gap between reading age and chronological age for children with learning difficulties in schools with different overall levels of achievement is shown. Children with learning difficulties in the lowest-achieving schools have average reading scores considerably lower than children in the higher-achieving schools. However, the trend in reading achievement of children with learning difficulties does not extend above the average levels of school achievement, and there is virtually no difference between the two higher-achieving groups of school.

The categorization of children as having learning difficulties, and other types of special educational need, reflects both difficulties experienced by pupils and the perceptions of these difficulties by teachers. One of the issues we have been concerned with is the extent to which teachers make these judgements relative to the context in which they work, and the extent to which teacher judgements are consistent across very different achievement settings. The differences between the proportions of children regarded as having special needs in schools with different achievement levels, indicated in the top row of Table 4.7, is an indicator of judgements being made in a way that is not just relative to context. The differences in median reading scores of children with learning difficulties in different schools is compatible with an element of relativity in judgements: children in higher-achieving schools being regarded as having a problem in learning when they would not be so regarded in lower-achieving schools. However, the differences also reflect the difference in the population eligible to be placed in the 'learning difficulties' category, and the similarity in scores across the two higher-achieving groups of schools does not suggest a strong element of relative judgements.

Teachers' and headteachers' views on aspects of special educational needs

The previous two chapters were based on teachers' descriptions of pupils in their classes with special educational needs, together with other data on various characteristics of schools and pupils. We were also concerned with teacher views on a number of broader educational issues in the area of special educational needs. In the present chapter we are concerned with teachers' views with regard to inclusion or integration, teachers' views on the location of the causes of various difficulties experienced by children, and expectations about the extent to which children's difficulties will be overcome. The data presented here are based partly on direct questions of a general nature on these issues in the interviews, and partly on inferences from what teachers told us about particular children.

INCLUSION

A major theme of current thinking about special educational needs is that of inclusion: the education of all children, whatever their difficulties, within the same neighbourhood schools. Terminology in this field has undergone a change in the last few years. In the Warnock Report (Department of Education and Science, 1978) and in influential research studies such as Hegarty and Pocklington (1981), the term 'integration' was used to describe the move towards educating all children in mainstream schools. More recently the term 'inclusion' has been used for this process. It is not always clear what is added to the debate by the change in terminology (see Croll and Moses, 1998 for a discussion). However, as used by some proponents of inclusion, there is a new emphasis on the changes which mainstream schools will have to make in order to be inclusive educational environments for all children, and on the necessary developments in curriculum, pedagogy and values, often of a very radical kind. In contrast, some discussions of integration looked only on the question of location: where children with special educational needs are to be educated rather than the nature of this education. (Although both the Warnock Report and studies such as Hegarty and Pocklington's included thoughtful discussions of types of integration similar to much of the arguments about inclusion.)

While there is a considerable degree of commitment in principle to the policy of inclusion, the practical implications of such a commitment are far less clear. For example, all the local authorities in the present study, and in other related research, have special education policy statements committing the LEA to the fullest possible inclusion. Nevertheless, some of these authorities have increased the proportion of children in special schools over recent years (Croll and Moses, 1998, 1999). The recent Green Paper on special educational needs, *Excellence for All Children* (Department for Education and Employment, 1997), reflects the tension in current thinking. The Green Paper includes a strong commitment to the principle of inclusion but at the same time talks of the importance of specialist provision for some children.

It is worth noting that the issue of inclusion is very much more prominent in the field of special education than it is in educational discussion more generally. While this is not surprising, it does highlight the potential limitation of moves towards inclusion. Thinking about inclusion has gone a great deal further in the special education sector than it has in the mainstream, but the issue is essentially one for mainstream education rather than for special education. In describing a study of education professionals' responses to inclusion we have noted that while it figured very substantially in the thinking of teachers and headteachers in special schools, and LEA officers with responsibility for special educational needs, it was much less a feature of discussions with headteachers and teachers in the mainstream. A theme of many of the discussions with people in special education was that, although many of them supported inclusion, they saw the continued necessity for special schools principally in terms of the limitations of mainstream provision (Croll and Moses, forthcoming).

In the present study we have addressed the question of inclusion from the perspective of mainstream schools in two ways. First, in the interviews, headteachers and teachers were asked explicitly if they thought separate special schools had a continuing role and, if so, for what sort of needs and for how many children they were appropriate. Second, in the discussions about individual children with special educational needs, teachers were asked about the provision the child needed and whether a placement other than in the regular classroom would be appropriate. In the 1981 survey, teachers were also asked about their attitudes to what was then called 'integration'. Responses were generally cautious, but it was noticeable that the teachers were much more positive about the integration of children with physical or sensory impairments than they were about children with serious learning difficulties or, especially, emotional and behavioural difficulties. Some such comparisons will also be possible in the current survey.

Virtually everyone in the 48 mainstream primary schools in the study believes that there is a continuing role for separate special schools. As the figures in the top row of Table 5.1 show, all of the headteachers interviewed, and all but a very small proportion of class teachers, held this view. To this extent the 'strong' programme of inclusion has not influenced the thinking of primary teachers. Perhaps more surprisingly, the results also show that many more teachers and headteachers think that a greater number of children should be going to special schools than think that fewer children should be in separate provision. One in three class teachers and rather over half of headteachers think that more children should go to special schools than do so at present. In contrast, well under one in ten of either the teachers or the heads think that fewer children should be attending special schools.

Table 5.1: The future of special schools: headteacher and teacher responses

	Headteachers %	Teachers %
A continuing role for special schools	100	98.3
More children should attend special schools	54.2	33.0
Fewer children should attend special schools	8.3	6.1
Special schools are needed for:		
Children with emotional and behavioural difficulties	66.7	69.4
Children with severe learning difficulties	35.4	58.2
Children with physical handicaps	25.0	20.4
Children with sensory difficulties	0	2.4
N =	48	294

Table 5.1 also shows the kinds of difficulties for which teachers and headteachers think that special schools are most appropriate. In the interviews this question was approached in an open-ended way rather than by prompting the interviewees with particular difficulties. Overwhelmingly, emotional and behavioural difficulties emerged as the predominant reason for children attending separate schools. Over two-thirds of those interviewed nominated emotional and behavioural difficulties as a reason for children not being in the mainstream, and this was very consistent across heads and teachers. The other category to emerge strongly was that of severe learning difficulties, which were mentioned by more than half the teachers and about a third of headteachers. Other difficulties were mentioned much less frequently: physical disabilities by a quarter of heads and a fifth of teachers, and sensory difficulties not at all by heads and by a very small proportion of class teachers.

The responses to questions about inclusion in primary schools were largely pragmatic ones (Croll and Moses, 1998). Teachers and heads were very conscious of the pressures of class sizes and resources which they were already under and stressed the problems they would have in coping with greater levels of difficulties. They were especially concerned with how they could meet the needs of other children in the class if they had children with serious special educational needs. This was especially so in the case of children with emotional and behavioural difficulties who were seen as disrupting the education of other children in an unacceptable fashion. However, there was also a concern with the best environment for children with special educational needs themselves. Special schools were seen as places with special expertise and special resourcing where these children could have their needs met appropriately. These two elements – a pragmatic concern for the realities of contemporary mainstream primary schools and a concern for the particular individual needs of some children – are similar to the perspectives to emerge from special education professionals in the study discussed above (Croll and Moses, 1999). However, the question of inclusion is much less a prominent issue in mainstream than in special settings, and the principled commitment to inclusion as an ideal, however distant, which was apparent in special education was much less evident in the mainstream settings.

The views on inclusion expressed in the current study show a continuity with the views expressed by teachers in 1981. In the earlier survey there was a considerable degree of caution about integration. The children with special educational needs who were seen as most likely to be successfully integrated in mainstream schools were those with physical and sensory impairments. The children seen as least likely to be successfully integrated were those with emotional and behavioural difficulties and, to a lesser extent, children with serious learning problems. This pattern emerges again in the present study. Children with emotional and behavioural difficulties were cited by a substantial majority as demonstrating the continuing need for special schools. Children with physical impairments were very much less likely to be mentioned in this connection, and children with sensory impairments were hardly mentioned at all.

The discussion above is based on explicit questions in the interviews about inclusion and the future of special school provision. A further perspective can be obtained from the discussions with teachers about particular children in their classes who had special educational needs. The questions about particular children were not about inclusion in general, or as an educational principle, but addressed the issue of what the teachers thought was right for a particular child in the current context of their class and school. As part of a series of questions about the nature of the child's needs and the provision being made to meet them, the teachers were asked if the mainstream class was the best place for the child, and if not, what sort of placement would be preferable.

As the figures in Table 5.2 show, for the overwhelming majority of children with special educational needs in mainstream schools, the teacher felt that the regular classroom was the right place for the child. In nine out of ten cases the teacher said that the child should be in the regular classroom, in just over one in twenty cases the teacher would have liked the child to be in a special class or special unit within a mainstream school, and in just under one case in twenty the teacher thought the child should be in a special school.

Table 5.2: Teachers' preferred placements for pupils with special educational needs

	All CSEN	Stage 2 and below	Stage 3	Stage 4 and 5	EBD
	%	%	%	%	%
Mainstream class	89.7	94.5	80.0	60.0	81.5
Special class/unit	5.8	3.4	12.1	19.3	10.1
Special school	4.4	2.2	7.9	20.7	8.4
N =	2,069	1,589	330	150	735

Of course, about a quarter of all children in the schools in the study were on the Register of special educational needs so the teachers were talking about a substantial minority of their pupils. It is therefore not surprising that special schools were not seen as appropriate in the great majority of cases. However, the figures for the preferred placement for children at different Stages of the Register confirms this relatively positive approach towards mainstream placement. As would be expected, the teachers are more likely to think a special class or special school is an appropriate placement as children move up the Stages of the Register. At Stage 2 and below, a special school is only seen as appropriate for about one in 50 children with special educational needs. At Stage 3 this has increased to about one in twelve, and at Stages 4 and 5 to about one in five of the children.

These results should be put in the context of the extent of the special needs which children at Stages 4 and 5 have. Currently over 40% of children with Statements of special needs are in special schools, and many of the children at Stages 4 and 5 in the schools in the survey would be in special education in some circumstances. But for 60% of these pupils the class teacher felt that the mainstream class was the correct setting, and for only 20% was a separate special school thought appropriate.

As we would expect from the earlier results, emotional and behavioural difficulty is a factor in teachers' views on the appropriate placement for pupils in their classes. The last column of Table 5.2 shows that having an emotional and behavioural difficulty very much increases the likelihood that the teacher will think that a child should not be in the regular class. But even in these cases, for the great majority of children with emotional and behavioural difficulties the teacher feels that the mainstream is appropriate.

The teachers in the survey were aware that special schools might be an option for some of the children in their classes, even where they thought the mainstream was the best placement, In the case of 7% of children on the special needs Register the child's teacher said that the needs were serious enough for a special school to be a possibility. However, for about 40% of these children the teacher thought that despite the extent of their needs the child belonged in the regular class. A particular theme of discussions over where the child should be educated was that of social needs and the child's own feelings. For example, teachers would often say that the main reason for a child remaining in a mainstream class was because she or he was happy there. Children were sometimes described as being appropriately placed because they were 'social' members of the class, even where they were not learning in the same way as other children and had different curriculum and teaching experiences.

The perspective on inclusion to emerge from the mainstream primary schools in the study differs somewhat between the general interview and the discussion of particular children. Mainstream primary teachers and headteachers are virtually unanimous in seeing a continuing role for separate special schools. Many think that there is a case for expanding that role. This belief is based mainly on a pragmatic sense of the existing pressures on mainstream schools and the perceived impossibility of teaching a mainstream class and at the same time meeting certain sorts of special educational needs. Children with emotional and behavioural difficulties are particularly seen as problematic in this regard. However, in considering the educational placement of children with special educational needs currently in their classes, teachers nearly always feel that the regular class is appropriate. Even where children have Statements, or are being assessed for Statements, in the majority of cases teachers want the child to remain in their class. There is no commitment among the teachers in the survey to inclusion as a generalized educational ideology, and there is a strong awareness of the pragmatic case for special schools to reduce the pressures on the mainstream. But, at the same time, there is a good deal of inclusive practice in the classrooms in the study, with teachers committed to meeting very considerable levels of educational needs in the mainstream.

TEACHERS' VIEWS ON THE AETIOLOGY OF SPECIAL NEEDS

In the 1981 survey we wanted to elicit teachers' perceptions of a variety of aspects of the special educational needs of the children in their classes. We argued that the perceived origins of the needs could affect how teachers thought and felt about their pupils and how they interacted with them in the classroom. We went on to place the teachers' perceptions in the context of possible explanations provided by social science in general and educational research in particular. In the 1998 survey we also obtained data from teachers about their perceptions of the causes or origins of special educational needs. During the teacher interview, after we had discussed the nature of the child's special needs and talked about the type of provision that was needed and what was actually available, we asked, in all relevant cases, the open-ended question, 'Why do you think this child has learning difficulties?' and, 'Why do you think this child has emotional and behavioural difficulties?' The teachers' answers were recorded and later a coding frame was devised to reflect their responses. Teachers were not presented with pre-coded categories and the results are intended to reflect as accurately as possible their own explanations.

As is to be expected, the pattern of answers between 1981 and 1998 showed a mixture of consistency and change. There was considerable similarity between the types of explanation provided, but interesting differences in the frequency with which various explanations were used. In 1981 the term 'special educational needs' was relatively new. Although it had enjoyed limited usage since the 1960s it was the Warnock Report that brought it to prominence. The term had an immediate resonance with teachers. One of the major findings of the original study was how close the match was between the Warnock estimate of the incidence of special educational needs based mainly on epidemiological studies (e.g. Rutter *et al.,* 1970), and the perceptions of primary schoolteachers based on their own professional expertise and experience. Teachers clearly felt that the concept of special educational needs linked with their own thinking and experience. Teachers were also, for the most part, prepared to offer explanations relating to the causes of their pupils' learning difficulties and emotional and behavioural problems. In nine out of ten cases they were prepared to offer explanations for such difficulties.

Tables 5.3 and 5.4 indicate the range and frequency of the explanations offered. Concentrating first on the data for 1981, it can be seen that although a range of explanations is offered, sometimes more than one for the same child, it is illuminating to group most of these explanations under one of three headings. This summary information in relation to the aetiology of learning difficulties is presented at the foot of the table. It is apparent that in 1981 teachers attributed over 70% of learning difficulties to a range of factors which together could be described as 'within child factors'. The most frequently cited was IQ/low ability but these also included 'attitude', 'lack of concentration', behaviour and general unspecified characteristics ('that's what he's like'). The second most common group of explanations were connected with the child's home and family background. These were considered to be a reason for learning difficulties in 30% of cases. In contrast, factors directly relating to the school and to teaching were offered as explanations for only a little over 3% of the instances of learning difficulty.

It appeared that, in 1981, teachers' explanations were dominated by factors related to children's innate and individual qualities and characteristics of their homes and parents rather than to characteristics of their schools and teachers and the teaching methods that were used.

Table 5.3: Teacher explanations for learning difficulties

		1998 %	1981 %
(a)	IQ/ability	20.5	43.8
(b)	Attitude	5.8	8.5
(c)	Lack of concentration	8.9	5.1
(d)	Health and physical handicaps	4.4	2.6
(e)	Absence	8.0	3.8
(f)	Home and family	24.9	29.8
(g)	Behaviour	7.9	3.8
(h)	Specific reading difficulties	3.6	1.9
(i)	Other specific learning difficulties	3.8	*
(j)	English as a second language	4.0	3.8
(k)	Low confidence/self-esteem	7.1	*
(l)	Immature/'slow starter'	8.4	*
(m)	School/teaching	1.2	3.2
(n)	Don't know	21.5	9.0
(o)	Generalized 'within child'	*	19.0
N =		1,884	1,492

Summary

	1998 %	1981 %
Any 'within child' (a, b, c, g, k, l, o)	48.1	70.5
Home and family	24.9	29.8
School/teaching	1.2	3.2
Don't know	21.5	9.0

* Not coded

Table 5.4: Teacher explanations for emotional and behavioural difficulties

	1998 %	1981 %
Home and family	52.2	65.8
Generalized 'within child'	4.4	19.9
Learning difficulties	4.8	1.8
Specific reading difficulties	0.8	1.1
School and teachers	0.8	2.1
Health and physical difficulties	3.0	1.9
Immaturity	4.1	*
Other	3.8	0.1
Don't know	26.1	16.3
N =	756	872

* Not coded

The picture presented by teachers was that learning difficulties were generally regarded to have their origins in the innate characteristics of the individual child, with a substantial minority of cases having causal factors related to home and parents. In contrast, behavioural and discipline problems were seen as originating principally from the home and parental circumstances of the child. With both kinds of difficulty there was seen to be considerable overlap between these causal factors. The teachers attributed about four in five of the difficulties they discussed, and about nine out of ten of the difficulties for which they were prepared to offer explanations, to either a child's innate characteristics or his or her home and family. In some cases a combination of these factors was cited. In very marked contrast, only about three in 100 of the difficulties discussed were seen as deriving from schools or teachers.

As part of the discussion of these findings we considered it useful to set them in the context of social scientific theories and ideas about academic performance and problematic behaviour. We considered that the sorts of explanation for children's achievement and behaviour with which teachers were most likely to be familiar derive from the tradition of concern over the relative influence of the home environment and the child's innate qualities: the nature–nurture debate. There is a substantial body of research in this area: for instance, researchers investigating the criteria for, and the effects of, selection at 11+ were concerned to show that not only measured IQ but also a child's socio-economic background influenced success and failure in the selection process (e.g. Floud and Halsey, 1957; Halsey and Gardiner, 1953). Studies such as those carried out by the National Children's Bureau (Pringle *et al.*, 1966) describe the relationship between a complex structure of medical and intellectual factors to children's achievements as well as relating these factors to children's home conditions.

These approaches also dominated the still influential report of the Plowden Committee, *Children and their Primary Schools* (DES, 1967). The first substantive chapter of this report was entitled 'The Children, their Growth and Development' and was concerned with developmental differences among children, factors affecting physical and emotional development and the measurement of intelligence. The next section headed 'The Home, School and Neighbourhood' considered the impact of the children's home environment on school. In considering the impact of environment, Plowden, like Douglas (1967) differed from some of the earlier studies in putting particular emphasis on the effect of parental attitudes towards education, as opposed to the effects of the physical or material circumstances of the home on children.

Causal influences on pupils' school performance deriving from their innate characteristics or from their home circumstances or from interactions between them are, of course, beyond the control of the teacher. It is undoubtedly helpful for the teacher to know of the possible influence of such factors, but such recognition will not necessarily produce changes in teaching method. The 1970s saw the beginning of a different type of research which was more centrally concerned with directly educational influences rather than social and psychological influences in the broader sense. In the UK, the Lancaster Study (Bennett, 1976) and the ORACLE programme (Galton and Simon, 1980) both concluded that the teaching methods used by primary schoolteachers have a systematic influence on classes of pupils, so that classes taught in some ways progress at a faster rate than classes taught in some other ways. Mortimore and his colleagues (1988) also concluded that *School Matters*. Similar research in the US has concluded that some teachers do elicit better academic performance than others and that this is systematically related to the teaching methods they adopt.

The classroom studies, in particular, are sometimes described as having opened up 'the black box' of the classroom and investigated the connection between teaching and learning. This type of research, while not discounting the potential significance of other factors, focused attention on factors of possible causal relevance to pupils' academic performance which are within the control or influence of the school or the teacher. This approach to research is concerned with more directly educational influences rather than social and psychological influences in the broader sense. Studies of this kind emphasize the significance of teachers and teaching and have established that, despite many significant factors outside their control, schools can and do make a difference. On the one hand this emphasizes the influence and responsibility of teachers but at the same time it offers strategies for teachers to use to maximize students' learning. This research was not specifically concerned with special educational needs but, if 20% of pupils are so regarded, any research findings related to regular classrooms are certainly related to pupils who may be regarded as having special needs.

In 1981 it appeared that teachers had explanations for the vast majority of the special educational needs of pupils in their classes and that these explanations were based outside the classroom. Pupils were viewed as bringing special needs into the classroom from outside, thus presenting teachers with needs to be met and problems to be solved. The period between the two surveys has seen a considerable increase in studies relevant to the effects of schools and teachers on learning. These were just beginning to emerge at the time of the earlier survey when most academic studies of educational performance had a fairly close match to teacher perceptions in focusing on home and ability.

However, the period between the two studies has been character-ized not only by a new range of research evidence but also by a very considerable change in the way that such evidence is reported and interpreted. The 'School Effectiveness' movement has largely succeeded in shifting an agenda from the social determinants of edu-cational success to the role of schools and teachers in influencing differences in levels of pupil performance. Although researchers have not typically presented this in terms of 'blaming' schools and teachers, a culture of blame and a focus on the supposed failure of the educa-tional service has informed much public debate and government initiatives from both political parties in the 1990s. The creation of school league tables and the use of 'value-added' measures to make these better reflect school contribution to performance focuses attention on the role of the school with regard to both educational success and educational failure. Discussions of the role of poverty in explaining the poor educational performance of some children have been replaced by the claim that 'poverty is no excuse for educational failure'.

Although coming from a very different perspective to that of the School Effectiveness movement, radical proponents of much greater levels of inclusion have also put the spotlight on the failings of schools. These arguments focus on special needs as an indication of the failure of schools to respond appropriately to their pupils. The arguments about the difficulties some pupils experience and create, which many teachers have put forward as a reason for separate provision, become turned round to be indicators of the ways in which schools have to change to meet a full range of educational needs.

The present study offers a unique opportunity to consider changes in teachers' views on the aetiology of special educational needs in the light of the new developments in educational research and the changed political environment since the early 1980s. The figures presented in Table 5.3 show the differences between the explanations given by teachers in 1981 and 1998. These demonstrate both interest-ing patterns of similarity and of difference. It is immediately apparent that there has been only a limited amount of change in the range of explanations offered. Teachers were responding to an open-ended question, and the answers reflect the explanations which came from them, rather than in response to prompting.

But although the range of responses did not differ greatly, the frequency with which they were offered has. If we first consider the summary at the foot of the table it would seem that some striking changes have taken place. Teachers are now far less likely to attribute a child's learning difficulty to any sort of 'within child' factor. While this type of explanation was offered in 70% of cases in 1981, teachers in the more recent study explained 48% of learning difficulties as coming from within the child. The primary class teachers still accounted for nearly half of learning difficulties in this way, so the idea of learning difficulties being derived from child characteristics is still strong, but nevertheless much less dominant than it was. Home and family were also cited rather less frequently than in the past, although the reduction is nothing like as marked. On the other hand, teachers in the 1998 survey were not more likely to think that teaching, either their own or other peoples', or the school, either in the form of the pupils' current or past schools, contributed to the child's learning difficulties. In fact, the number of instances attributed to school factors actually fell from just over 3% to just over 1%. The reduction in the attribution of causality to 'within child' factors and to the home and family has come about through a reduced willingness to offer explanations rather than from a shift in the type of explanation offered. It was, perhaps, a surprising feature of the original survey that teachers were quite so willing to put forward explanations for what are undoubtedly very complex phenomena. The 1998 data may reflect a more realistic sense of this complexity and of the interplay of different elements and the difficulty of isolating them in accounting for learning difficulties.

More details are contained in Table 5.3, and a fuller picture of the range of explanations can be explored. If we first consider the changes in the use of the 'within child' factors to explain learning difficulties: Table 5.3 shows that considerably fewer than half as many instances of learning difficulties were attributed to 'IQ/ability' by teachers in 1998 as compared to 1981 (20.5%. as compared to 43.8%). Teachers are clearly not as likely to put a child's poor academic performance down to IQ. We are not concerned here with the 'real' reasons for a pupil's poor performance but with how teachers view the origins of the learning difficulties of pupils in their own classrooms. We are not arguing that teachers are becoming either more or less accurate in their views. Although fewer instances of learning difficulty are attributed to IQ, other 'within child' factors were cited. As in 1981, the teachers in the 1998 study considered that a child's attitude, lack of concentration, classroom behaviour and reading difficulties could also explain learning difficulties.

In 1981, 19% of learning difficulties were, in the teachers' eyes, connected with what we called 'generalized within child factors', instances where the teacher described a child as simply being 'like that'. In the second study this vagueness was much less apparent and three new types of explanation emerged. It is interesting to note, and possibly significant, that these new categories, 'specific learning difficulty other than reading', 'lack of confidence/low self esteem' and 'immature/slow starter', together account for 19.3% of explanations, whereas previously the generalized 'within child' factor was used in 19% of cases. The emergence of these new types of explanation indicates a subtler approach on the part of teachers.

The connection between self-esteem and achievement had not attracted much attention in 1981 but, more recently, self-esteem has become a focus of interest (Craske, 1988) and teachers' awareness of this is shown in their responses. In the second survey teachers considered that over 8% of learning difficulties were due to a child being immature or 'a slow starter'. The children in this study are at Key Stage 2 so, particularly those in Year 3 and Year 4, are young children. Children at this age who are immature for their age, or indeed young for their class, can have levels of performance that can be viewed as problematically below their peers; this can appear to be particularly acute when the child has yet to master basic reading skills. In 1981 teachers felt that, for a small number of pupils, having problems with reading was a cause of learning difficulties more generally. To reading difficulties teachers have now added other specific difficulties of a range of types, connected with both literacy and numeracy. This again indicates a more sophisticated approach.

The picture in relation to the aetiology of emotional and behavioural difficulties is rather different, though some similarities are also apparent. Details are presented in Table 5.4. As with the perceived origins of learning difficulties, teachers in the second survey were much less likely to regard any 'within child' factor as causal. They were also more likely to say that they were unable to offer any explanation; teachers were not prepared to speculate about the causes of well over a quarter of the emotional and behavioural difficulties of their pupils. By far the most frequently used explanation in both studies was 'home and family', although this possible cause was used less frequently in 1998 than in 1981 (52.2% compared to 65.8%). Pupils were seen as bringing these difficulties into the school which, if they were explained at all, were seen as likely to originate in home and family circumstances. Despite seeing emotional and behavioural difficulties as likely to have originated in the home, teachers were not necessarily critical of the parents (though they were in some instances). They often saw parents struggling to cope in extremely difficult circumstances. As in the case of learning difficulties, teachers saw the school and teachers as a possible cause of emotional and behavioural problems in very few cases in 1981 and even fewer, less than 1%, in 1998.

Overall, the picture is one of teachers regarding children having special educational needs which have originated outside the school and which they bring into the school to be ameliorated. When the causes of individual children's difficulties are discussed, teachers rarely felt that the school played any role in causing these problems. However, headteachers, talking in more general terms, painted a slightly different picture. Whatever the perceived aetiology of special educational needs, many headteachers thought that schools could help at least some special educational needs from arising. This is a position quite distinct from thinking that schools and teachers can make a positive contribution to alleviating special educational needs; if schools can take action to prevent special educational needs from arising, it would appear to follow that if they then fail to take action they, at least in some measure, are responsible for them.

Each of the headteachers was asked the question, 'Do you think that schools can play a major role in preventing special educational needs from arising?' In outline their responses consisted of 28 who considered that schools could play a major role in prevention, eleven who thought that they play some role and nine who felt that schools responded to special educational needs but could not prevent them. There was very considerable variation in the way heads thought about this issue and how they responded to the question; several heads with widely differing views clearly thought the question was hardly worth asking as the answer was patently obvious. These ranged from, on the one hand, the head who claimed, 'Of course schools can prevent problems from arising. What do you think schools are for?' to the equally emphatic, 'Oh no. We can't really prevent special educational needs; we can't control what happens out of school or change a child's basic ability, can we? What we can do is to respond as early and as effectively as possible.'

We also asked the heads about specific strategies that operated in their schools to prevent special educational needs arising. A wide variety of schemes was mentioned including Reading Recovery

Programmes, Whole School Behaviour Policies and Home/School Liaison Groups, but the type of scheme most frequently mentioned (by 37 out of the 48 heads) were Early Intervention Initiatives. It is not entirely clear whether or not early intervention is actually preventative. However, even if that is not strictly speaking the case, there is a widespread belief that the early identification of special educational needs and possible special educational needs can result in school action that can improve the learning potential of children, aid their emotional development and encourage them to be well behaved.

The responses of teachers and heads can be put in the context of the various arguments and research evidence on school effectiveness, pupil abilities and the social contexts of schooling. In comparison with the earlier survey, teachers in 1998 were less likely to attribute difficulties to innate characteristics of children or to their home and family circumstances. Nevertheless, these were still the attributions made for difficulties in the great majority of cases. As in 1981, teachers were very unlikely to attribute the difficulties of specific pupils to failures in schools and teaching, suggesting that a culture of blame has not been internalized by the teaching profession. However, a majority of headteachers, while very aware of the impact of socio-economic circumstances on the difficulties their schools faced, also thought that schools could put strategies in place which would, at least in part, alleviate these difficulties.

OUTCOMES FOR CHILDREN WITH SPECIAL EDUCATIONAL NEEDS

In addition to speculating about the aetiology of special educational needs, teachers were also asked what they thought the future looked like for their pupils with learning difficulties and emotional and behavioural difficulties. Table 5.5 indicates the extent to which teachers think pupils in their classes will overcome their current difficulties. Comparisons between opinions expressed in 1981 and those in 1998 can be made in relation to learning difficulties, but not emotional and behavioural difficulties. The table makes pretty dismal reading. Not only do teachers regard far more pupils as having learning difficulties than they did in 1981, they are quite as, if not more, pessimistic about these difficulties being rectified.

In 1981 class teachers thought that well over a quarter (27.4%) of learning difficulties would be completely overcome; that although this large number of junior-school-aged pupils were currently experiencing problems, they were temporary in nature and would not

Table 5.5: Teachers' views on the extent to which children will overcome their learning and emotional and behavioural difficulties

	1998			1981
	LD %	EBD %	LD and EBD %	LD %
Completely overcome	17.6	11.5	7.5	27.4
Partly overcome	56.3	50.5	54.4	40.4
Not at all	10.0	11.5	11.8	20.9
Get worse	6.1	11.5	12.3	–
Not sure	9.0	15.0	14.0	11.3
N =	1,884	756	577	1,898

become permanent. This number had fallen by 10% to 17.6% in 1998, indicating that teachers thought that a smaller proportion of the growing number of pupils considered to have learning difficulties would overcome their problems. On the other hand, they did think that well over half (56.3%) would improve to some extent and only 10% would not get any better. The same teachers thought that 6% of children with learning difficulties would actually get worse; a category of response that was not used in 1981.

The predictions for pupils with emotional and behavioural difficulties are quite as pessimistic. Although about half are expected to make some improvement, only 11.5% are expected to overcome their difficulties completely; the same number as teachers expect to get worse. The greatest pessimism, perhaps not unexpectedly, is reserved for children with a combination of learning difficulties and emotional and behavioural difficulties. Only 7.5% are predicted to completely overcome their problems, while practically a quarter (24.1%) are expected either to make no improvement or to actually get worse.

The implications of these views are not straightforward. It would perhaps have been encouraging to find teachers more optimistic, but there may well be a fine line to be drawn between optimism and realism. There is currently considerable political emphasis on the importance of teachers raising their expectations of pupils, and their views on the outcomes for pupils with learning difficulties and emotional and behavioural difficulties do not appear to be consistent with this. However, the question of the impact of teacher expectation on pupil performance is not resolved and the impact may be exaggerated. Certainly the schools and teachers are making considerable efforts to meet the needs of these children, as the evidence in the following chapter shows.

—6—

Provision for special educational needs in the mainstream school

The prevalence of special educational needs and factors influencing assessment have been considered in the previous chapters. The focus of attention in this chapter and the two that follow is on the ways in which schools seek to meet the needs of these children. Chapters 7 and 8 will deal with the management of special needs provision and with LEA policies as they impinge on schools. In the present chapter we are concerned with the experience children have of provision for their special educational needs. The data presented here are based on what class teachers told us about the provision made for specific children in their classes whom they regarded as having special needs.

As in the 1981 study, it is an overview of provision that will be presented, not a detailed account or analysis of different ways of teaching children with different kinds of special need or an evaluation of different work schemes. Following an analysis of the statistical data on provision we shall also present case studies of the provision for particular pupils, looking especially at different Stages of the special educational needs Register. While recognizing the importance of the whole range of special educational needs, it is provision for learning difficulties and, to a lesser extent, emotional and behavioural difficulties, which will be the focus of most of the discussion. As we have seen, these are by far the most numerous of the special educational needs in primary schools and the central issues of learning and behaviour dominate the teachers' and schools' perspectives on special needs. It is through a consideration of provision in these areas that issues of the nature of special needs and special provision and their connection with general educational issues can best be explored. Much less information is given on very specific types of help, especially support of a medical nature. This is partly because there is relatively little provision of this sort, even in a large survey. But it is also because such provision is usually not seen as educational and teachers, and even special educational needs co-ordinators often know little about it.

PROVISION FOR SPECIAL NEEDS: AN OVERVIEW

In Table 6.1 the levels of extra help and teacher feelings about further help are presented for 1998 and 1981. A number of interesting comparisons over time can be made from a consideration of this data. It is immediately apparent that not only has the proportion of pupils regarded as having special educational needs increased between 1981 and 1998, from 18.8% to 26.1%, but more of the nominated pupils are also receiving some sort of special provision. Although varying considerably in type and quantity, in the current survey nearly 80% of pupils with special educational needs are receiving some sort of 'extra' help. This is a considerable increase on the 56% in 1981. However, it is when the proportion of the total number of pupils in the Key Stage 2 classrooms receiving special help is compared that the differences in the levels of provision become particularly apparent. In 1981 just over one in ten of pupils were receiving extra help. By 1998 this number had practically doubled and now over one in five of all pupils are receiving extra help. Given this very substantial increase in provision, it is perhaps not surprising that the gap between what teachers want for their pupils and what they receive has, to some extent, narrowed. However, it is still the case that teachers would like 40% of their pupils with perceived special educational needs (10% of all the pupils in their classrooms) to receive more help than they are getting. It would appear that although the desire for more 'extra' provision may not be absolutely insatiable, it will be extremely difficult to satisfy. This is not altogether surprising within an educational context where it is difficult to accept that improvement is not possible. Even where standards are high and considerable effort is being exerted, there is always the thought that things could be better. It is also understandable that teachers who, for example, think that one session of withdrawal for extra help with reading is beneficial may well think that two sessions would be even better.

There are however some children who are not receiving help and for whom their teachers do not consider that it is required. Although this group is relatively small, it contains enough children for it to be of some significance, consisting of just over 15% of pupils regarded as having special needs and 4% of all pupils in the classrooms. The same phenomenon of pupils described as having special needs but neither receiving nor needing extra help was apparent in 1981. In the earlier

Table 6.1: Provision for pupils with special educational needs 1998 and 1981

	% nominated pupils		% total sample	
	1998	1981	1998	1981
Pupils receiving extra help beyond ordinary class provision	78.8	56.2	20.5	10.6
All pupils for whom teachers would like (more) extra help	40.1	44.2	10.4	8.3
Pupils not currently receiving extra help for whom teachers would like such help	6.0	21.8	1.6	4.1
Pupils either receiving extra help or for whom teachers would like extra help	84.8	78.0	22.1	14.7
Pupils receiving no extra help	21.2	43.8	5.5	8.2
Pupils receiving no extra help and teachers not thinking it is required	15.2	22.0	4.0	4.1
N =	2,123	2,317	8,149	12,310

survey a slightly higher proportion of children fell into this category than in 1998. The significance of these figures is that they highlight the ambiguity in the definition of the term 'special educational needs'. Since Warnock recommended the abandonment of the categories of handicap which, it claimed, put too much emphasis on what children could not do, in favour of special educational needs which emphasized what children required to learn, needs are defined in terms of provision; more precisely, in terms of 'extra' provision. A child has special educational needs if she or he requires 'additional' help. Nevertheless, teachers are operating within a perception of special needs where some children are regarded as having such needs but are not regarded as requiring extra provision. In these cases (and perhaps some others) teachers must be focusing on the problems pupils have rather than considering them in terms of additional needs.

As well as the definitional problem of special needs not requiring special provision there can also be considerable difficulty in some cases in establishing the distinction between ordinary classroom provision and extra or special provision. In 1981 the issue of exactly what constituted special provision was addressed and subsequently defined as:

anything beyond the ordinary teaching activities of the classroom. It includes extra help given by the teacher at lunch time or break, remedial reading taught in a separate class and attendance outside the school at, for example, a child guidance clinic or reading centre. Also included are a small number of instances where the ordinary classroom activities of the child have been devised according to specialist advice such as that from an educational psychologist or remedial reading specialist. Thus defined, special provision varies from something which is a very small part of a child's school day and of which, in some instances, he may not be aware, to a very extensive special provision such as the help of a full-time auxiliary or daily attendance at a reading centre. (Croll and Moses, 1985, p. 93)

This definition raises a number of interesting points. First, basically the same definition of special provision is still relevant and the same difficulty of what exactly can count still applies: this is particularly the case when the child does not receive help in addition to what is provided in the classroom by the teacher but does, at least to some extent, do differentiated work, prepared with very varying degrees of expertise. As in the first study we were primarily concerned with teachers' perspectives and so we regarded as 'special' provision anything that the child's class teacher regarded in this way. When discussing individual pupils and their special educational needs with teachers we asked, 'What sort of special help is the child receiving? Does this include: help within the classroom; help involving withdrawal from the class but in-school; help provided out of school?' Details of the help given were recorded under these major headings. For the most part these questions elicited detailed and unambiguous answers, but things are not quite so clear-cut when it comes to descriptions of class teachers' own classroom practice. When class teachers said that they themselves offered special help to pupils with special needs in their classrooms these activities, whatever form they took, were recorded as 'special help'. However, it is possible that of two teachers engaging in the same classroom practices, one would regard what they did for a child as 'special' and the other would not. This is another indication of the lack of clarity that surrounds special educational needs provision and indeed the whole concept of special educational needs.

THE NATURE OF SPECIAL PROVISION

In 1981 most additional special educational needs provision involved 'remedial reading'. The teaching of reading is still a major concern in special educational needs provision in the primary school, but the term 'remedial' has almost totally disappeared. This is another example of the continued influence of the recommendations of the Warnock Report which considered this term unsatisfactory because of its perceived perjorative overtones and the lack of accuracy in its description of many of the activities which it encompassed. The out-of-school Reading Centres mentioned in the quotation from the report on the 1981 survey have also disappeared. This type of provision has disappeared partly as the result of LEAs looking for economies – and this type of separate centre was often expensive to run – but also because of an increasing desire to provide for all children within their own school. At a time when the desirability of withdrawing pupils from the classroom for extra help was increasingly being called into question, it seemed unsatisfactory, as a matter of principle, to actually send pupils out of school, regardless of the quality of the provision that was being offered. In 1998 teachers reported that only 5% of children with special needs in the study received help of any sort in centres outside the school. These invariably offered very specialist help: speech therapy, child guidance, various types of medical help and similar provision.

In Table 6.2 various aspects of the special provision received by pupils in 1998 are presented. Data are given on the curriculum areas for which children receive help, the people who are providing the help and the type of teaching context in which help is given. The table gives these details for all sorts of help received by children. It also gives details separately for help received in the regular class and for help for which children are removed from the classroom. The question of withdrawal from the regular class will be considered in more detail later in this chapter, and the present discussion is simply concerned with similarities and differences between in-class and out-of-class support. All children appear in the first column of the table and at least one other column. Many children appear in all three columns.

The first part of Table 6.2 presents the curriculum areas in which children are receiving help (curriculum being defined very broadly to include 'behaviour' and 'care'). Although the terminology of special needs support has changed since the 1981 survey, the picture is very similar with regard to the major areas in which support is given. The term 'remedial reading' is no longer used and the term 'literacy',

Table 6.2: The nature of special help in 1998*

		All help %	In class %	Out of class %
Help with:	Reading and literacy	76.0	63.1	75.9
	Number	31.1	28.3	18.8
	Behaviour	8.9	8.0	5.2
	Care	0.8	0.5	1.1
Help from:	Class teacher only	40.0	60.7	1.4
	Special educational needs co-ordinator	7.1	2.0	9.6
	Support teacher	31.0	3.1	48.8
	Learning support assistant/ classroom assistant	40.2	29.8	34.1
	Volunteer/parent	4.8	4.2	2.6
	Other	5.8	4.7	3.6
Context:	One to one	26.8	14.3	29.3
	Group	54.9	26.3	66.3
	Other	18.3	69.4	4.4
N =		1,673	1,306	1,015

* Percentages will not always sum to 100 as there may be multiple responses

which was not widely used before, is commonplace. It is this area, however described, which dominated extra provision in 1981 and still does so. Three-quarters of all children getting any sort of additional help are getting help with some aspect of reading and literacy. For these purposes we are considering all aspects of what can be loosely described as 'literacy' together, but teachers' descriptions of this sort of provision were frequently much more specific. Although reading was most commonly mentioned, spelling, writing, composition, phonic awareness training, sequencing and work on specific literacy schemes were also referred to. Reading and literacy were the dominant feature of both support within the regular class and support when children were withdrawn from the classroom. However, it was even more a feature of out-of-class provision than it was in-class.

The second most frequent curriculum area in which children got additional support was numeracy. Just under a third of all children who were getting additional support were receiving help with numeracy. This was a more common feature of in-class support than it was of support outside the regular class. As we saw in Chapter 3, learning difficulties dominate teacher perceptions of special educational needs and the basic skills of literacy and numeracy dominate the perceptions of learning difficulties. These are the areas where support is given both within and outside the classroom. The pattern of provision reflects the pattern of identification of special needs in that provision for reading and literacy is very much more common than provision for numeracy.

Other sorts of support for children which were mentioned by teachers were help with managing behaviour and various forms of care. These were very much less likely to be part of special needs provision than is help with learning. Rather less than one in ten of children receiving additional help are receiving help with behaviour, most usually in the classroom. This only partly reflects the greater level of learning difficulties than emotional and behavioural difficulties. While the ratio of behavioural problems to learning difficulties is about 1:2.3, the ratio of provision for these difficulties is about 1:8.5. There is no doubt that emotional and behavioural difficulties present schools and teachers with many problems, and well over half the children with such difficulties were also described as presenting their teachers with discipline problems. But schools struggle to make specific provision for such difficulties, partly because, unlike most learning difficulties, it is difficult to see what such provision should be. This difficulty of finding a way to meet such needs may partly explain the teachers' views on appropriate placements discussed in the previous chapter. Teachers were more than twice as likely to feel that children with emotional and behavioural difficulties should be educated outside the regular school or classroom than they were for other children with special educational needs.

When children are withdrawn from the classroom for special help it is usually quite clear what activity is taking place, who is providing the help and how long it lasts. When help is provided in the classroom the situation is often not quite so specific and the exact nature of the special help may be less clearly defined. The data from Table 6.2 indicate that many more children receive some sort of 'extra' help in the classroom than details are provided for. Some of the special help given in the classroom is, to all intents and purposes, the same as withdrawal: a small group or an individual child is involved in an activity somewhat different from the rest of the class. However, special help may take a number of different forms. The data reflects teachers' views of special help and teachers may, or may not, regard the fact that a child has an Individual Education Programme as constituting provision, or differentiated work, or 'having just a bit of extra attention'. (The 1981 survey, which involved systematic classroom observation, showed that class teachers did in fact give more attention to pupils who they thought had special educational needs.) This type of provision may be just as, or more, effective as that which is much more specific but is much more difficult to clearly identify. It also shades into more general considerations of classroom teaching where the distinctions between special educational needs issues and general pedagogical issues merge, in the same way as the distinction between children who do have special educational needs and those who do not are not definitive.

This issue is particularly apparent in the figures presented in Table 6.2 for who provides the additional help and the context in which it is provided. Overall, extra help is given by the class teacher, learning support assistants or classroom assistants and support teachers. Little direct support to children is provided by the special needs co-ordinators, and little by volunteers and parents or others. (The category 'other' includes both visiting non-teaching specialists and other teachers in the school, often the headteacher.) The figures for the class teacher have been included only when the class teacher is the only source of special support in that context (i.e. in or out of class). In 60% of the cases where children are getting support within the classroom this is only from the class teacher. Almost no out-of-class support is provided by the class teacher. As we suggested earlier, in the case of this kind of support it is very difficult to distinguish between 'extra' help for a child and the ordinary process of the teacher responding to each child's needs.

Support teachers may be working for an LEA support service or directly for a school. (The teachers interviewed were frequently unaware which was the case.) They work almost entirely outside the regular class and about half of the pupils getting support out of class were working with a support teacher. Learning support assistants and classroom assistants (the terms were both used in interviews) work both in and out of class. Just under one-third of children getting in-class support and just over one-third of children withdrawn from the classroom were working with a learning support assistant. Special needs co-ordinators are not heavily involved in supporting children, but when they do so this is nearly always on the basis of withdrawal from the classroom.

Table 6.2 also gives figures for the kinds of educational settings in which children get additional help. In the case of withdrawal from the classroom this is fairly easy to interpret: support is either in a small group or individually in a ratio of about two to one. Within the classroom this is much harder to interpret. Small groups are more common than individualized support, but there is a very large 'other' category. This mostly reflects the difficulties of clearly defining the kinds of additional help given by the class teacher.

The broad overview of support for special educational needs can therefore be summarized as a combination of in-class and out-of-class support and a combination of class teacher, support teacher and learning support assistant support. A majority of children get support within the classroom but this is mainly just from the class teacher. About 40% of these children get other in-class support, mainly from a classroom assistant or learning support assistant in a mixture of one-to-one and small-group situations. About half of all children with special needs are withdrawn from the class for support. In about half of cases this is work with a specialist support teacher, in about 10% of cases with the special educational needs co-ordinator, and in just over a third of cases with a learning support assistant. About three-quarters of all children getting help are getting it for reading and literacy, with a minority getting help with numeracy.

WITHDRAWAL FROM CLASS

The withdrawal from the classroom of pupils with special educational needs was an almost universal practice in the schools in the survey. Only one school, a very small country primary school with only one child with special needs, did not practise withdrawal. However, it was much more widespread in some schools than in others. The proportion of children with special needs withdrawn for some part of the week ranged from under 5% to over 90%, with an average of just under 50%. One-third of the schools had no definite policy on providing 'extra' help for pupils by withdrawing them from the classroom. Decisions were made about what would be best for the child in each particular case and, although those involved in the decision might favour either in-class support or withdrawal in principle, a definite school policy did not determine what action was taken. Most schools, however, regard withdrawal as an issue that they need to address explicitly, and two-thirds of the headteachers reported that a policy was in operation in their schools. Half of these policies were firmly in favour of withdrawal and the heads describing this position considered it a practice that was beneficial to children, often speaking in terms of the benefits of one-to-one and small-group work in a quieter and more intimate atmosphere that suited some children. The rest of the heads were less enthusiastic about the practice and 15% were positively opposed. Even with a strong preference to keep all activities within the classroom, schools find that, although they can reduce it to a minimum, there are instances where children may still have to be withdrawn, particularly where help is provided by an outside agency and withdrawal is their usual way of working.

The extent to which children are withdrawn from the regular class for special help with learning difficulties and a comparison with the 1981 figures can be seen in Table 6.3. In 1981, 57.3% of pupils with learning difficulties were withdrawn from the classroom for extra help: 8.8% of the total number of pupils in the study. In 1998, although the proportion of pupils with learning difficulties withdrawn had fallen to 51.7%, because of the increase in the number of children regarded as having learning difficulties, the proportion of all children withdrawn from the classroom has actually risen to 11.9%.

Table 6.3: Pupils with learning difficulties withdrawn from the classroom 1998 and 1981

	1998		1981	
	% of pupils with learning difficulties	% of all pupils	% of pupils with learning difficulties	% of all pupils
	51.7	11.9	57.3	8.8
N =	1,884	8,149	1,898	12,310

Although a large number of children with learning difficulties do spend time withdrawn from the classroom, it is unusual for this type of provision to dominate the week. In 1981 we concluded that the amount of withdrawal experienced by children in the study was not sufficient to regard it as forming the basis of an alternative experience of schooling. For 80% of the pupils withdrawn, this form of provision amounted to, at the most, a little over a tenth of their school experiences and in most cases rather less. For fewer than one in 50 of children withdrawn for special help did this special provision approach one-half of their time in school.

It can be seen from Table 6.4 that the change between the two surveys has been towards less time spent outside the classroom. Although a rather higher proportion of pupils in Key Stage 2 classrooms are withdrawn at some point during the week, very few are withdrawn for long; in fact just over half are withdrawn for an hour a week or less, and a further fifth for between one and two hours; under 6% spend more than five hours a week outside the classroom. For this small number of children there is a serious question about the similarity and difference between their experience of schooling and that of other children. This is a serious issue for the education of these particular children, but it is difficult to see how the amount of withdrawal experienced by most children can amount to an alternative experience of schooling. The main issue here is one of efficacy; if withdrawal is most effective it is the best way to proceed, but if offering support in class is the most effective then that strategy should be pursued. As with most controversial issues surrounding special educational needs provision, there are no definitive answers to this question.

When withdrawn, children are in small groups of rarely more than six and more usually between two and four, though it is not unusual for a child to get one-to-one teaching. As the figures in Table 6.2 showed, most withdrawal in this study was in small groups; this was the case in about two-thirds of instances, while children were taught individually in about one-third of cases. This represents a considerable amount of individual attention and serves to emphasize the individualized nature of the concept of special educational needs.

Table 6.4: Length of time spent out of the regular class for help with learning difficulties: 1998 and 1981

| | % pupils withdrawn | |
	1998	1981
30 minutes or less	8.4	3.9
30 minutes to 1 hour	46.7	20.1
1 to 2 hours	19.3	36.4
2 to 3 hours	10.8	20.4
3 to 5 hours	8.9	15.0
5 to 10 hours	5.3	2.5
10 hours+	0.3	1.7

SUPPORT AT DIFFERENT STAGES

As we should expect, the extent of support for children with special educational needs increases as children move to higher Stages of the Register of special educational needs. This reflects both the increasingly severe nature of the difficulties experienced by children and the way that Stages of the Register usually trigger additional resources for children. Although the increased resourcing of higher Stages seems in some sense natural and inevitable, it was not necessarily accepted as such in schools. As the data from special educational needs co-ordinators, discussed in the next chapter, show, a significant number argued that it would be more appropriate to concentrate resources at Stages 1 and 2 when later problems might be averted. Similar views were expressed by some of the class teachers.

Nevertheless, as the figures in Table 6.5 show, there is a fairly consistent progression in levels of support across the Stages (figures are not given for Stage 4 as this is a transitional Stage where schools were often not clear what they should be providing). The extent of support from someone other than the class teacher increased from a third of pupils at Stage 1 to virtually all pupils at Stage 5. (The one exception was a child whose serious medical problems had resulted in a Statement but who did not have immediate educational difficulties.) The proportion of children withdrawn from the classroom for support increased from a quarter at Stage 1 to two-thirds at Stage 5 and a slightly higher level at Stage 3. When children were withdrawn, the amount of time they spent outside the classroom also increased across the Stages. Children at Stage 1 who were withdrawn spent an average of 1.2 hours outside the classroom and this increased to 1.8 hours for children at Stage 3. There was then a considerable increase, with children at Stage 5 being out of the classroom for double the Stage 3 level.

Table 6.5: Special provision and stages of the Code of Practice

	Stage 1	Stage 2	Stage 3	Stage 5
% help from other than class teacher	33.2	66.7	78.8	99.2
% withdrawn from class	25.4	59.5	73.5	67.5
Average time withdrawn from class	1.2 hours	1.6 hours	1.8 hours	3.7 hours
N =	856	744	339	120

TRAINING AND SUPPORT

It is striking from the figures presented above that it is the class teacher who is most frequently the provider of support for children with special educational needs. Consequently, their skills and knowledge are of paramount importance. In 1981, when the concept of special educational needs was still new, only 20% of class teachers reported that they had received any sort of training directly relevant to special needs. The increased awareness generated by the Warnock Report, and then the 1981 Act and its implementation, raised expectations of increased levels of training and competence. It was thought realistic that, through training, especially in-service training, the level of expertise in schools would be substantially increased and the need for additional specialist provision much reduced (Hegarty and Moses, 1988; Mittler, 1993). Many more of the class teachers in the 1998 study had attended some sort of in-service course connected with special educational needs, although the figure of 45% is still less than half of all teachers. Two-thirds of these courses were short courses run by the LEA and were of a general nature, often dealing with issues like the introduction of the Code of Practice; three-quarters of courses had been attended since 1993. Relatively few dealt with specific areas such as learning difficulties, emotional and behavioural difficulties or sensory impairment. Fewer still led to any sort of qualification; only 4% of teachers had qualifications such as a certificate or diploma in special educational needs. On the one hand it could seem that too few primary teachers have specialist training but, on the other hand, it could be argued that if they have good general teaching skills they will also be good at teaching children with special needs.

Next to class teachers it is classroom assistants and learning support assistants who offer the most help. Whereas class teachers almost always provide help within the classroom, the help provided by support assistants is divided almost equally between the classroom and withdrawal. Every school, even the smallest, used support assistants to help provide for pupils with special needs. The range of support assistant hours across the schools ranged from two hours to 240 hours a week, with an average (inasfar as this is meaningful) of just over 49 hours, which represents a considerable amount of school staff time. Support assistant time is often specifically allocated to individual children, usually on Stages 3, 4 and 5, and just over a third of heads said that all their support assistance time was for specific children. However, it is clear from the information from teachers on the help provided for individual children that support assistants were often deployed in a much more general way.

Not all schools could call upon the help of support teachers to provide for special needs. Thirty-seven per cent of heads said that their schools had no hours of teaching time specifically allocated to special needs teaching. In these schools provision was made by class teachers with the help of support assistants. Among the 63% of schools which did have some sort of extra teaching help, the level of provision varied very considerably. This ranged from just one hour a week to 52.5 hours, the equivalent of close to two teaching appointments. Most of the special needs teaching hours were provided by what heads described as 'specialist' teachers; over a third of the schools had this type of help and another fifth had a part-time teacher who mostly did special needs work but was not concerned exclusively with this type of teaching. A much more unusual arrangement was for class teachers to have a specific allocation of hours which released them from class teaching to concentrate on special educational needs.

The help provided by both support assistants and support teachers can be funded in a variety of ways, but at the level of working with children these differences are not apparent. Both types of support staff can be full- or part-time members of the school staff, either resourced from a special needs supplement or not; or they may be attached to support services which may charge schools for their services or may be centrally funded by the LEA and offer services free to schools. Typically, schools will have some support provided through a special needs supplement but will often also provide additional help themselves. It is not at all unusual for the same individual to be funded from different sources; in effect to have two jobs but to actually have one consistent role working in the same school.

Despite increasing concern over both overall levels of provision and how the funding is divided, the basis of the support provided is less clearly understood at classroom level than it used to be. When asked to describe the type of help given to an individual child, teachers were not necessarily able to say whether a support assistant or teacher was a member of the school staff or from a support service. Perhaps the main point of interest here is how little this matters from a teacher and pupil perspective as opposed to a managerial view. In 1981 it was possible to say how many children were receiving help from 'out-of-school resources', mainly the support services. In principle it may still be possible to do this, but the situation is much more complex and cannot be accurately approached from the classroom.

There was a role for parents and occasionally other volunteers. The

overall figures are low here as most schools do not make these arrangements. However, a very small number of schools make more extensive
use of the services of parents. Helping to provide 'special' help is
rather different from most parental activities in schools and there
would appear to be special circumstances surrounding most instances
of parental involvement in special needs provision. The most usual
case is parents who are helping their own children under the super-
vision of the special educational needs co-ordinator or class teacher
and, more unusually, a parent or volunteer with educational qualifications who are, in effect, doing a professional job unpaid.

EXAMPLES OF PROVISION FOR PUPILS ON VARIOUS STAGES OF THE CODE OF PRACTICE

From the statistical analysis of the teachers' accounts of the provision
made for their pupils with special educational needs it has been
possible to create an overview of the type and level of support that is
typically available to Key Stage 2 pupils with various special educational needs and on each stage of the Code of Practice. The following
short accounts of the provision made for a number of individual
children give an idea of what support actually looks like for pupils
and teachers.

Example 1: Brian on Stage 5 with a Statement

Brian is an 8-year-old boy with general learning difficulties and speech
and language problems. He has difficulties with classroom learning
and his teacher particularly mentioned problems with reading and
associated skills but did not think that these problems could be
described as dyslexia. He has a reading age over two years behind his
chronological age which in a child of this age means that he is only
just beginning to read; but he does achieve a score on the reading test
and is not a non-reader. Nevertheless Brian's teacher thinks that a
special school would be a realistic alternative for him although she
feels that 'a nurturing unit in our school would work best for him'.
Although his teacher did not think that Brian suffered from emotional
and behavioural difficulties she did feel that he was painfully shy and
very afraid of failing and that this made it particularly difficult to
overcome his learning difficulties.

As would be expected in the case of a child such as Brian, his class
teacher has consulted with the full range of people who are responsible for his assessment and the organization and delivery of his special
help: the special educational needs co-ordinator, headteacher, other

class teachers, staff from the Learning Support Service and the support teacher and the educational psychologist. She is also in regular contact with Brian's parents, in fact she sees his mother every day.

Brian gets a considerable amount of extra help both in the classroom and through withdrawal. In addition to the routine provision made by his class teacher, Brian gets two hours help each week from a support teacher in the regular class. This teacher offers help with all aspects of learning and works with the child on a one-to-one basis. The teacher likes this sort of special help and would like more hours. In addition to this very intensive individual help he also takes part, in a small-group setting, in three different withdrawal groups. He goes to two hour-long 'English' sessions with a special educational needs teacher; four one-hour sessions of 'Maths' taken by another class teacher, and one 45-minute session of 'Social Skills', again with the school's special needs teacher. The 'Social Skills' group is a rather unusual provision but one that this particular school is enthusiastic about. The head felt that many of the younger pupils in particular lack social skills training at home. The sessions that the school provided both addressed some of the problems that are actually manifested by the children and performed a very effective preventative function. Brian's teacher thinks that he has speech and language difficulties but he does not appear to receive *specialist* help in this area. However, the extra individual and small-group help he is getting will be useful in this respect.

Brian's class teacher is relatively optimistic about his future progress. Although she thinks that he is likely to continue to experience some difficulties with learning, she thinks he will partly overcome his difficulties and that he is likely to move to a lower Stage on the Register before the end of the year.

Example 2: Debbie on Stage 5 with a Statement
Debbie is an 11-year-old girl in her last year of primary school. She has been the subject of a Statement since her first year in school but her present teacher does not think that a special-school place was ever seriously considered for her and still thinks that she should be in a mainstream school and in a regular classroom. Debbie does however have serious difficulties. Her teacher describes her as having general learning difficulties, with poor skills in all areas and a major memory problem. Although she is 11 years old her reading age is only a little over 6 which means she is only just starting to read and is very seriously behind her peers. She also has a very limited vocabulary which her teacher feels constitutes a language problem, although this

is not mentioned on her Statement. In addition, she has emotional and behaviour problems: her teacher finds her very difficult to communicate with and, at times, she is very difficult to control in the classroom. Debbie comes from a very disturbed background where she probably gets very little encouragement and appears not to be very well cared-for physically. The family are known to social services, who have been in contact with the school about her welfare. Her teacher thinks that her emotional and behavioural difficulties are the result of her home background and that her difficulties are, at least in part, the cause of some of her difficulties with learning. Debbie also suffers from a physical disability but her teacher does not know very much about it. She has a very pronounced limp which makes running and strenuous exercise very difficult and she gets tired very quickly. This condition does not directly impinge upon her other difficulties but is another reason why she is not a thriving child.

The class teacher, the special educational needs co-ordinator, the educational psychologist and Debbie's mother have discussed her progress and provision for her needs, but her mother has only come to the school once this academic year. Debbie gets quite a lot of extra help but not of a specialist kind. She gets twelve hours in the classroom either one-to-one or in a small group, and a further five hours withdrawn from the class for one-to-one help, in both cases by a classroom assistant rather than a specialist support teacher. Debbie's teacher thinks that she will make progress but is concerned about what may happen to her if her home circumstances deteriorate any further.

Example 3: Katy on Stage 4

Katy is currently in the process of being assessed and her teacher expects that this will result in a Statement for her. The exact nature of her difficulties, their likely origins and the appropriate provision are creating great concern and uncertainty for her teacher. Katy is described as having general learning difficulties and has a reading age two years behind her chronological age. It is however her other problems that are causing the most concern. She needs to wear glasses but absolutely refuses to, which has a considerable effect on her school work. Her teacher describes her as possibly autistic but feels that he does not have the expertise to make that judgement. She is described as a very 'unusual' child who exhibits extremely 'odd' behaviour both at home and at school. She suffers from what appear to be 'panic attacks' and she also has a very strong and serious desire to be a boy. Her teacher, however, does not think that a special school would be a realistic alternative and considers that a mainstream school and the regular classroom is the right place for her.

How to provide for her needs is however a difficult problem. The class teacher has talked to Katy's parents and to the special educational needs co-ordinator and to the head and, recently, to the educational psychologist who was reported as being 'very concerned about her'. Both the school and the parents are currently awaiting the outcome of the professional assessment which they hope will identify the exact nature of the problems and recommend a programme of provision. In the meantime Katy is not receiving much extra help. She could benefit from extra help with reading, but school policy is to provide this type of help in withdrawal groups, an arrangement which they feel works well; but Katy simply refuses to take part. It is highly likely that the Statement will specify some sort of support for reading, but in the meantime she is not getting any help. The only assistance she is getting is what can be provided by a support assistant who is actually allocated to another child but who copes with Katy's panic attacks.

This is not because of any reluctance to provide but because of not knowing what to do. Teachers often want advice on provision and more often think a child would benefit from getting more of what they are actually getting. It is unusual for a child's needs to be so difficult for teachers to assess. Cases like Katy's do, however, occur from time to time and schools need expert help to enable them to adequately provide.

Example 4: Trevor on Stage 3
Trevor's teacher thinks that he has a number of special educational needs. He has general learning difficulties and although he is not regarded as having a specific reading problem, at 8½ he still does not score on a reading test. Trevor's teacher says he has emotional and behavioural difficulties and often creates discipline problems both in the classroom and in the playground. His behaviour is considered to be an important, though not the only, cause of his learning problems. When he was younger he had hearing difficulties but his hearing is now supposed to be normal although the teacher is not convinced about that. He also has some speech problems, particularly the pronounciation of vowel sounds, which may be connected. Trevor also suffers quite badly from asthma. His teacher thinks that his needs are such that special school would be a realistic alternative and actually thinks that he would be better off there.

Despite the severity and the multiplicity of his perceived needs he is being offered only a limited amount of extra help. Although he is on Stage 3 which is thought appropriate to his special educational needs the provision made is rather less than is usually associated with Stage 3. The special educational needs co-ordinator and the school's special educational needs teacher have consulted with the class teacher about Trevor and his parents have also met with the teachers, but the support services have not been involved; any help that Trevor receives has to be found from the school's resources. In the regular classroom he gets differentiated work in all areas of the curriculum so, in some respects, he could be seen as getting constant special help. He also gets help in a small withdrawal group once a week for an hour for 'spelling' and twenty minutes a week individual attention for 'reading', both with the special educational needs teacher.

Trevor's teacher does not regard the help he is getting as adequate, though he does not want more help for him in his present school. He is pessimistic about his future and thinks his difficulties are likely to get worse. He thinks that Trevor's best hope lies in attendance at a special school but that is not on the cards in the foreseeable future. He is likely to stay on Stage 3 with the current level of support but, at least in his teacher's view, that will not really be enough.

Example 5: Michael on Stage 3
Michael has general learning difficulties but his teacher thinks that he also has a specific reading problem. He is in the lowest of three sets for maths. He does cope but at 10 years old has a reading age of just over 7 years. He has no other difficulties and is described as 'a likable boy with supportive parents'. His lack of progress in reading does sometimes get him down and his teacher is concerned about this and thinks that this could possibly lead to problems in the future if he does not make progress with his reading. Like most children with special educational needs there is no question of special school and his teacher thinks that adequate provision can be made for him without a Statement.

Michael's class is divided into sets for many 'literacy' and 'numeracy' activities and Michael takes part in all the maths groups and some of the literacy groups. Within the context of the group activities, the teacher says that she keeps a special eye on Michael together with the other children with special educational needs. The class has a learning support assistant who is attached to a child with a physical disability who has a Statement. Her time is used flexibly in the classroom and she often helps other children, including Michael, who are in the same group as her Statemented child. He receives more specialist help in withdrawal groups spread throughout the week. He gets help for three 40-minute sessions with a support teacher from the Learning Difficulties Support Service and two 40-minute sessions from a learning support assistant who works to a programme arranged by the support teacher. Michael's teacher feels that this level of support is probably sufficient to meet his needs and she thinks that he will make progress.

Example 6: Gary on Stage 2
Gary is on the special educational needs Register because of learning difficulties and emotional and behavioural difficulties which can result in classroom behaviour that causes problems for his teacher. Gary has a reading age eighteen months younger than his actual age of 9½; he does not receive any additional help but his progress is being monitored and his teacher feels he will make progress. The real problem is his behaviour which does affect his learning. A special school is not thought to be at all appropriate. His teacher thinks that he comes from a very unsettled background but has never met his parents, despite frequent attempts to do so. Gary's teacher has talked to the special educational needs co-ordinator about Gary but this has not resulted in any real strategy to address his behavioural problems. They think that some form of counselling may be appropriate but feel that his problems are not acute enough to consider child guidance, and no one on the school staff has the relevant training or experience. What Gary's teacher realistically hopes for is some ancillary help in the classroom to help contain the worst of his behaviour.

Example 7: Melanie on Stage 2
Melanie is described as a girl of rather below-average ability and school achievement whose parents, frequent visitors to the school, are disappointed in her accomplishments. She is in her last year at primary school and is both young for her class and immature for her age. Her reading age is about eighteen months behind her chonological age and, because she is young for her class and because the overall standard of her class is well above average, her performance appears worse in this classroom than it would in many others.

After consultation between teachers, the special educational needs co-ordinator and the parents it was decided that Melanie should attend two small withdrawal group sessions each week taken by the school's special educational needs teacher. Her parents would like her to get more help but her teacher thinks this level is sufficient and that she will make progress, even if not as far or as fast as her parents would like.

Example 8: Ian on Stage 2
Ian is 10½ and he is on the special educational needs Register because he is dyslexic. He does not have any other difficulties; he is a bright boy who is doing very well in some aspects of his school work and, even in literacy skills, he is not far behind his chronological age with a reading age of 10. Despite not being behind his year group, the apparent unevenness in his abilities and the difficulty he had with reading in particular, despite a great deal of effort and supportive parents, resulted in the school and the parents asking for an assessment from the school psychological service. The result of this assessment was a diagnosis of dyslexia and consequently Ian started to receive three and a half hours one-to-one help with a support teacher in daily sessions. Ian's parents felt that this level of help was inadequate but the school and the LEA felt unable to provide more resources for a child of Ian's level of difficulty and considered that he was actually receiving sufficient help. Ian's parents contacted the Dyslexia Institute which now works with the school on Ian's reading provision, and Ian also has extra help from a private tutor out of school hours from the Dyslexia Institute. Ian's teacher thinks that he will partly overcome his difficulties and that, to a great extent, he already has. There are likely to be remaining difficulties but he will learn to cope with them.

Example 9: Ahmed on Stage 1
Ahmed is on the special educational needs Register because he has mild celebral palsey and the school and his parents feel that he needs 'a close eye kept on him'. This takes the form of such things as making allowances for him in terms of time and presentation of written work, understanding that he is not good at PE, though he does take part, and being watchful in the playground in case of bullying – though this is not in fact thought to be a problem as Ahmed is a popular boy. He does not have learning difficulties and in his final year of primary school has a reading age in excess of 12½.

Example 10: Lucy on Stage 1
It is not clear exactly why Lucy is on the special educational needs Register. She does not have any obvious special needs but her teacher feels she is perhaps not making the progress that she might. She is coming to the end of Year 4 and she is a reasonably competent reader, but her spelling is not as good and she makes lots of small mistakes in writing. She does not get help in addition to the differentiated work

in the regular classroom, but her teacher regards this as special provision and feels that it is probably sufficient to meet her needs. Her progress is being carefully monitored and her parents are seen regularly.

Example 11: Anne on Stage 1

Anne is 8 years old and is on the special educational needs Register because she has a specific learning difficulty. Her reading age matches her chronological age but she struggles badly with maths and her teacher feels that her difficulties are acute enough for Anne to be regarded as having special educational needs and needing extra help. Anne's difficulties have been discussed by her teacher, the special educational needs co-ordinator, the head and her mother and grandmother. Anne's teacher feels that her difficulties are mainly due to a lack of concentration. She is currently getting extra help through going to a small withdrawal group once a week with a class assistant, and her teacher feels that she would benefit from more of this kind of help. At the moment the teacher thinks that she will probably only partly overcome her difficulties.

Example 12: David on Stage 1

David is a 10-year-old boy who arrived in his present school towards the end of the previous term and so is still new to the school. As far as his teacher knows he was not on the special educational needs Register at his last school, though he finds this difficult to believe. He considers David to have general learning difficulties and to have very serious emotional and behavioural difficulties; one aspect of which is that he is extremely difficult to control in the classroom and is very aggressive towards other children in the playground. At lunchtime he creates problems for the 'dinner ladies' who have complained about him. David's teacher says that the school in general and his classroom in particular are very orderly places and the general standard of behaviour among pupils is very high. Consequently, many other pupils find David's behaviour particularly distressing.

David was put on the special educational needs Register a few weeks after he arrived at the school. His teacher and the special educational needs co-ordinator have seen his parents once but they know nothing about his home circumstances and would like more contact with his parents. The school does not routinely test children's reading so there is no reading age for David, but his teacher says that he has poor reading skills. Although he does have learning difficulties it is his behaviour that is the real cause for concern. His teacher feels that he ought to have a Statement and that he ideally should be in a special school both for his own good and for the good of the other children in his class. He probably will move up a Stage on the Register but his teacher feels that getting him Statemented will be a long uphill struggle.

At the moment he is only getting a very limited amount of extra help because he is only on Stage 1 and will have to move to a higher Stage for more resources to be made available. He does differentiated work in the classroom and is withdrawn by a classroom assistant for one session a week to receive help with his writing and spelling. This is the type and level of additional help that the school usually provides for a pupil on Stage 1, but David's teacher feels that it is inadequate to meet his learning needs, let alone improve his behaviour problems. These needs are so acute that he feels that the school will not be able to meet them adequately, and a special-school place should be found for David.

—7

The management and organization of special needs provision

The last chapter gave an overview of the level and type of special educational needs provision found in the 48 schools in the study, and brief accounts of the provision made for individual children with a range of special educational needs gave an idea of what provision actually looks like. The point was made that, from the perspective of the classroom, it is not always clear how the 'extra' support that children and their teachers receive is organized. It is not of any great importance whether, for example, the support assistant or the support teacher or the in-service provision for the special educational needs co-ordinator is funded from the school's delegated budget or comes directly from centrally held LEA funds. Nevertheless, the issue of the allocation of resources is viewed as being of great importance by the headteachers and by the LEA officers responsible for special educational needs. If the overall amount of money available for education was larger, then exactly how particular types of provision are resourced would probably be less important. As it is, the implications and possible implications of different types of resourcing are highly significant. Both at school and LEA level there is a finite pot of money, and if it is spent on one type of provision it cannot be spent on another. This can mean not just that one type of provision is better funded than another but that the resourcing for the less well-funded provision will actually be inadequate. In this climate, the management of resources is very important.

The complex issue of the division of responsibility between LEAs and schools and the variety of forms that this can take is considered in the next chapter. Here the focus of attention is on the organization of provision at school level, although this cannot be done without some reference to LEA policy and practice. The LEA has retained more control and has more direct responsibility for provision for special educational needs than it has in other areas of education. There is considerable variation in policy and practice between LEAs, but there are perhaps three main areas of activity where the policy of the LEA most directly affects schools: the fixing of the overall level of the school budget and the determination of the constituent parts of the budget; the funding of provision for pupils with Statements; and the provision of support services including the school psychological service.

THE BUDGET

Over three-quarters of headteachers said that their school's delegated budget included some sort of special educational needs supplement; that is, the formula used by the LEA for calculating the schools budget included a factor or factors designed to reflect the level of special educational needs in the school and its funding in addition to that based directly on pupil numbers. Although the intention behind such a supplement is that it should be used for special educational needs provision, because it is part of the budget *delegated* to schools, it can in fact be used for whatever purposes the school wishes. It is indicative of the complexity and confusion surrounding resourcing for special educational needs that some of the heads who claimed that their schools did not receive a special educational needs supplement were in LEAs where the officer with responsibility for special educational needs produced detailed documentation showing how the supplement was calculated.

From the earliest days of the Local Management of Schools scheme there were fears that special educational needs would be starved of funds (Evans and Lunt, 1993). There is no evidence from the present study that this is happening. There is a lack of understanding of the budget on the part of some heads, and some instances of poor communication between the Education Office and particular schools, but this appears to result in dissatisfaction with the level of resourcing and with LEA policy and procedures, rather than in the schools making inadequate provision for special educational needs. The schools appear to be committed to providing for special educational needs, but sometimes feel that they are doing this from their 'own' resources whereas they should be getting 'extra' from the LEA. This position is well illustrated by the following quote from a head worried about possible cut-backs in funding:

Currently the LEA are supporting six hours of special educational needs support teaching and 25 hours of non-teaching assistance after very strenuous representations from the school, but they are not committed to continuing this funding and the school on its own will have to make provision, but there will be no special allocation or budget. The LEA seem unlikely to give support other than to those on Stage 4 or above.

In other words, those who would ordinarily attract support anyway.

Only ten of the 48 heads felt that their school had adequate resources to meet the special needs of all their pupils. These ten schools were spread across different authorities so there is no hint that any particular authority is particularly good at satisfying its schools. (The sample of schools and authorities is, in any case, unsuitable for drawing any firm conclusions of this type.) Although there was considerable variety in the sort of extra provision mentioned by heads (some of it very specific to the circumstances of the individual school), perhaps not surprisingly, more specialist support teachers and more support assistants were frequently mentioned. However, it was more general teaching staff that were mentioned most frequently: 41.6% of headteachers who felt they needed additional resources wanted more teachers. This is interesting because it serves to further emphasize that meeting special educational needs is, for the most part, the 'ordinary' business of 'ordinary' schools requiring 'ordinary' resources.

The desire to provide more for children with special educational needs was also expressed by class teachers, not just in general terms but specifically in relation to individual children in their classes. Overall they would like 40% of their pupils with perceived special educational needs to receive more help than they are currently getting; that is 10% of all the pupils in Key Stage 2 classrooms in the study. Just over 20% of the pupils with special educational needs were not getting extra help; the majority of these pupils, approximately 70%, were, not surprisingly, either on Stage 1 or not on the Register at all. Most of the rest were on Stage 2, while a small number of unusual cases were on higher stages. It was, on the whole, pupils on the lower Stages for whom teachers wanted more help.

Table 7.1 gives some indication of the wishes of teachers, but when considering the data displayed in the table it is important to bear in mind how these figures were generated. They are based directly on teachers' responses to an open-ended question. Class teachers were asked to describe the nature of any special help given to each child and were then asked, 'Is there any other special help you would like for this child?' Teachers were able to answer in whatever way they saw fit, but their responses were almost certainly more restrained than

Table 7.1: Characteristics of additional help wanted by class teachers

Nature of additional provision	% for whom extra help was wanted
Help with any aspect of literacy/reading	21.9
Help with mathematics	3.0
Help with EBD	7.8
Help in small group	18.7
One to one	22.6
Help from support teacher	17.0
Help from LSA	35.4
Assessment	8.8
N =	851

would have been the case if they had been presented with a 'wish list' from which they could choose.

There is no one type of provision that is mentioned very much more frequently than any other; teachers' desires vary according to the pupils concerned, what they are already getting and their own preferences. However, there are a number of points worth making. The most frequently mentioned area of the curriculum is reading and associated skills; in comparison, maths is infrequently mentioned. As there is far more help actually offered in the area of literacy than in maths, this would seem to emphasize yet again the predominance of reading in the primary classroom. Teachers would also like more help from support assistants; this was in fact the most frequently mentioned form of extra help, and mentioned twice as often as additional help from support teachers. It is possible that this stated preference may have more to do with the perceived availability of help rather than a real preference for one type of help over another in more ideal circumstances. There was a small number of pupils (8.8%) whom teachers thought needed more provision but did not know what form it should take, and they thought that what was required was an expert assessment.

STATEMENTS

Despite having emphasized the 'ordinariness' of most 'special' provision, there is a small number of children perceived as requiring considerable amounts of special help if they are to flourish in mainstream primary schools. If these children are given the protection of a Statement of special educational needs they are then guaranteed a particular amount of special help. In the previous chapter the levels of help provided to children on the different Stages of the Code of Practice were described and the difference between the resources given to Statemented and non-Statemented children was very apparent. The number of pupils for whom it is appropriate to write a Statement is an issue of great concern to most LEAs, particularly because of the cost implications, and is frequently an area of tension between local authorities and schools.

The schools in the study varied considerably in the number of pupils they had with Statements; seven schools (14.5%) did not have any children with Statements, half had either one, two or three, and no school had as many as ten. The LEAs may be concerned about the overall numbers of pupils with Statements for whom they are responsible but, from the perspective of the individual primary school, the number of children involved is very small. Bearing in mind these small numbers in each individual school and the resource implications, it is not surprising that 62.5% of the heads thought that more children in their school should be Statemented. One head replied that she thought that about two children in each of the school's eight classes would probably benefit from having a Statement. This sort of response would appear to indicate the desire to acquire more resources for special educational needs provision in general through Statements. However, other heads wanted far fewer (never more than six) and spoke in terms of particular children, including those who were in the process of assessment. Their desire for more Statements was focused on the perceived needs of individual children, not primarily as a mechanism for acquiring more resources; although they were, of course, aware that more resources would follow.

Possibly because of this close connection between perceived needs of particular children and the Statementing process, with the possibility of not being able to provide as they would have liked for a child, heads were frequently critical of the whole Statementing process. Only eight out of the 48 heads felt that the practices in operation in their LEA were satisfactory; the other 40 were all critical. The two most widely voiced criticisms were, what they perceived as unnecessary bureaucracy with a particularly heavy burden for schools and, associated with this, undue delay. Many were keen to point out the benefits of early intervention while, they claimed, the LEA appeared to obstruct this by using delay as a policy.

Heads were also asked whether they thought that any of the children in their school with Statements would have their needs more appropriately met in a special school. Twenty-one (44%) thought that their school was the best place for all their Statemented pupils but the majority (56%) felt that there were pupils who would be better off in a special school. This has serious implications for the implementation of a policy of inclusion because it indicates that, whatever may be thought in principle about the desirability of inclusion, there are children currently in primary schools whose headteachers feel, at least with the current level of resourcing, they would be better provided for in a special school.

The headteachers were generally critical of their LEAs; all but four wanted to see changes in policy and practice in relation to provision for special educational needs. Perhaps inevitably the desire for more resources topped the list, but this was not the only area mentioned. As in the case of Statementing, there were numerous complaints about how long the various processes took. Heads described the difficulties in establishing when the school was able to claim help from support services to assist with provision for pupils on Stage 3 of the Code of Practice or to get advice and/or assessment for children. Some heads saw this as a deliberate tactic, aimed at discouraging schools from seeking additional resources, rather than a case of inefficiency or under-capacity. A small number of heads expressed concern over a particular problem they were currently facing which did not necessarily reflect what they thought in general about LEA policy and practice. This is nevertheless significant as provision is for real, individual children at a particular point in time; not hypothetical children in hypothetical circumstances. About a quarter of the study's headteachers wanted substantial or fundamental changes in their LEA's policy and procedures. In particular they wanted more consultation over these matters and they wanted a clearer view on what the LEA policy actually was. Although these feelings were fairly general, they were particularly acute in the new unitary authorities which were recently established and so in very unusual circumstances.

THE ROLE OF THE SPECIAL EDUCATIONAL NEEDS CO-ORDINATOR

A key feature of provision for meeting special educational needs in mainstream schools is the role of special educational needs co-ordinator. This role was created following the 1993 Education Act, although, of course, in many schools it was an extension of existing roles rather than an entirely new one. According to the Code of Practice the co-ordinator is responsible for:

- the day-to-day operation of the school's special educational needs policy;
- liaising with and advising fellow teachers;
- co-ordinating provision for children with special educational needs;
- maintaining the special educational needs Register and records of children with special educational needs;
- liaising with parents of children with special educational needs;
- contributing to the in-service training of staff;
- liaising with external agencies.

Some of the implications of this extremely wide and demanding remit are considered by Davies *et al.* (1998), and the complex legal context of this work is discussed by Evans (1998).

In the present study, interviews were conducted with special educational needs co-ordinators in 46 of the 48 schools. These dealt with their training and the time they had available for the role, the operation of the Code of Practice in their schools and, in particular, how children moved between Stages of the Register of special educational needs, their contacts with various support services and their feelings about various aspects of their role.

Most commonly the co-ordinator's role was taken by a class teacher who performed the role in addition to her or his ordinary teaching responsibilities. Only a minority (15.2%) of the 46 co-ordinators interviewed spent all their time dealing with special educational needs, combining the role with being a specialist special educational needs teacher. A further six (13.2%) of the co-ordinators were also the headteacher. This was a particularly common arrangement in the smaller schools, and in such schools the headteacher/special educational needs co-ordinator often also had class-teaching responsibilities. Three of the co-ordinators were also deputy heads and, for the remainder, just over 70%, their main responsibility was teaching a mainstream class.

Table 7.2 presents the time involved in the special educational needs co-ordinator's role by giving figures for the amount of time allocated to the role and the co-ordinator's estimates of the time involved in performing it. (Of course, these figures involve combining amounts of time from schools of very different sizes.) Time allowances for the role are fairly low, especially so in the context of the list of responsibilities contained in the Code of Practice. Just under four out of ten co-ordinators have no time allowance, and just over four out of ten have five hours a week or less. Only a small minority have more substantial time allowances than this. Of the six headteachers who act as co-ordinators, five are in the 'None' category for time allowance which slightly distorts this figure. But the great majority of the co-ordinators with no time allowance are ordinary class teachers.

The co-ordinators' estimates of the time the role takes are presented in the second column of Table 7.2. Not surprisingly there is a disparity between these figures and the figures for time allocation, although perhaps not to the same extent that some accounts of the role would lead us to expect (e.g. Davies *et al.*, 1998). Over half of the co-ordinators are spending five hours a week or less on the role, while only one in five is spending more than ten hours a week. These figures are, of course, much higher than the proportions of co-ordinators with a time allowance on this scale. However, more than half of the co-ordinators are operating on a basis of the equivalent of an hour a day or less, and the great majority are operating on two hours a day or less.

Table 7.2: Time for special educational needs co-ordinator's role

Hours	Time allocated %	Time spent %
None	39.1	0
Up to 5 hours	43.5	52.3
More than 5 and up to 10 hours	8.7	27.3
More than 10 hours	8.7	20.5
N =	46	46

All of the special educational needs co-ordinators had received training either directly in the role or in various aspects of special educational needs. However, only a minority had any qualification in special educational needs. Two-thirds had received specific co-ordinator training and many had been on courses concerned with reading difficulties, learning difficulties generally, and emotional and behavioural difficulties. For most, these were not substantial enough courses to lead to qualification, but seven had diploma- or certificate-level qualifications in special educational needs, and one had a masters degree.

The Code of Practice lists the responsibilities of the special educational needs co-ordinator but these will not necessarily reflect the practical reality of what they do and what is important to them. During the interview the co-ordinators were asked what they saw as the most important aspects of their role. This was an open-ended question without prompting about different parts of the role, and the responses give a picture of how co-ordinators see the role and what is important to them. The areas to emerge from the interviews mirror fairly well the responsibilities laid out in the Code of Practice, although there were additional areas covered and variations in emphasis. Fifteen of the 46 co-ordinators mentioned maintaining school records, the Register of special educational needs and other aspects of formal documentation as an important aspect of their role, and a further four mentioned Individual Education Plans. Advising and supporting colleagues was an important aspect of the role, mentioned by twelve co-ordinators. A further six put this on a more systematic basis and said that they were concerned with staff development and in-service training. Other aspects of the role which reflected the Code of Practice were liaison with parents (ten) and liaison with outside agencies (seven).

An area which was described as important by about two-thirds of the co-ordinators was that of management, monitoring and taking a whole-school overview. There was clearly a common area of concern in many such comments, although with varying emphases on different aspects of the role. Some emphasized the monitoring of the progress of individual pupils as crucial, with a stress on ensuring that needs were being met and progress being made. The phrase 'making sure that no one slips through the net' or something similar was used by several co-ordinators. For others the emphasis was more on whole-school issues and co-ordination of provision across the school. This was expressed both in terms of taking an 'overview', explicitly mentioned by nine co-ordinators, but also in terms of direct intervention, 'making things happen', 'making sure support happens'. Other sorts of managerial roles such as managing learning support assistants and managing resources were mentioned by nine of the co-ordinators.

Other aspects to emerge from the interviews which are not explicitly in the Code of Practice were working directly with children, advocacy for special educational needs and keeping up to date with new developments and new approaches. Eight of the co-ordinators said that they regarded their direct work with children as the most important part of what they did as a co-ordinator and another said that she would have liked that to be an important part of the role. Work with children was sometimes conducted within the classroom alongside the child's teacher but was more commonly on the basis of withdrawal from the regular classroom either individually or in small groups. An advocacy role with regard to special educational needs in the school was mentioned explicitly by three of the co-ordinators, and similar comments with regard to the visibility and degree of priority given to special needs emerged elsewhere in a number of interviews. Several were very pleased at the high profile special needs issues had in their school, while others were concerned to raise the profile and saw this as an important aspect of their role.

The comments by the co-ordinators on the aspects of the role which were important to them showed a variety of perspectives. However, this did not fall into any particular pattern, with variations occurring on a systematic basis. It is not possible to talk of different 'types' of special educational needs co-ordinator, although there are varying emphases. The roles that they saw as important are fairly close to those described in the Code of Practice, with a focus on co-ordination, monitoring, support and advice to teachers, liaison with parents and outside agencies, and maintaining records and the Register. Although there was some concern with meeting the formal requirements of the Code of Practice, the major issues were those of seeing that children's needs were met.

Although it was not possible to distinguish different co-ordinator 'styles', there was evidence of a tension experienced by some between the essentially managerial aspects of the role and the opportunity to use their personal expertise with individual children. From their perceptions of the most important part of their roles, it is clear that the co-ordinators in the schools in the study have accepted the managerial aspect of the role. They emphasize the importance of monitoring, of co-ordination, and records and other documentation. Nevertheless, many are in the role because of personal interests and skills in meeting special needs. There was a frustration, clearly felt by some, that managing a school's special needs provision was less fulfilling than using their expertise with children.

A number of further perspectives on the role and approaches to special educational needs in mainstream schools emerged from the interview data. These partly reflect fairly predictable concerns over time and resources and the demands of paperwork. However, they also reflect views on the appropriate strategies for meeting special educational needs and on recent policy developments. As we have seen, there is a disparity between the amount of time special educational needs co-ordinators have allocated for the role and the amount of time it takes. Thirteen drew attention to this problem and talked about the 'excessive demands of the job' and the conflict with other demands on their time. Headteachers who were also co-ordinators were particularly likely to find it conflicting with other demands. Several people argued for the role to be a full-time one, and others would have liked more time so that they could use their expertise to work directly with children. In addition to the concern with time, a further eight mentioned resources more generally as a problem. These included secretarial support with the extensive records and documentation, but also appropriate materials and teaching resources and time for in-service training. The extent of the paperwork involved in the procedures for dealing with special needs was also a concern to a number of co-ordinators. Some people were highly critical of the procedures, to the point of arguing that 'getting the documentation right is regarded as more important than helping children'. More commonly, they expressed support for the Code of Practice in principle and saw the more systematic approaches to monitoring and recording special needs as valuable but, at the same time, often felt that the 'form-filling has got out of hand'.

Other aspects of the co-ordinators' perspectives related both to strategies and to policy. Early intervention and strategies for the prevention of special needs were seen as important by many. In some cases they argued that the way in which the progressive Stages of the Register of special educational needs generated further resources was counter-productive. They felt that more resources could often be better targeted at Stages 1 and 2, where intervention might have genuinely remedial effects, rather than at Stages 3 and above which the formulae operated by most LEAs envisaged. Other views on strategies included some reservations about the effectiveness of in-class support. There were two aspects to this concern. One was that they felt withdrawing children for special help was a more effective strategy than in-class support and that in some schools this was being under-used. The second was a concern over the quality of support provided to children by classroom assistants and learning support assistants. Several co-ordinators felt that these people had inadequate training to meet children's special needs and were concerned that the children who most needed a teacher's support were spending a lot of their time in class with someone who was not a trained teacher.

Policy issues raised in the interviews included the government initiatives on literacy and numeracy and the perception of a pressure to further inclusion of children with more serious special needs in mainstream schools. The Literacy Hour, in particular, was mentioned as a negative influence on providing for special educational needs and as conflicting with the co-ordinator's view of what children with learning difficulties needed. Inclusion was also seen as a problem for mainstream schools. In the case of most sorts of difficulties this was mainly seen as a resource issue rather than opposition to inclusion in principle. Children were seen as being placed in mainstream classes without the transfer of resources to support this. However, in the case of children with emotional and behavioural difficulties, there were often reservations about such placements in principle.

The special educational needs co-ordinator is responsible for keeping the special educational needs Register. At a minimum this involves the recording of pupils who come onto the Register and keeping details of the provision made for them and their progress as they move either up or down between Stages or leave the Register; but it can also involve the administration of tests and other assessment procedures, the development and reviewing of Individual Action Plans, liaising with class teachers and support assistants, a wide range of support services and parents. There is wide variation in the amount of time, both official and unofficial, that co-ordinators spend on their special educational needs activities, and this will affect the role they can play.

Procedures used for recording information about pupils with special educational needs vary widely between LEAs and between individual schools. Whatever the details of the system, it requires a good deal of effort to make it work, principally on the part of the co-ordinator; but all members of staff are involved. Perhaps rather surprisingly, there was considerable support and a fair amount of enthusiasm among class teachers for their school's system of record-keeping. Ninety per cent of teachers were happy with the system they used, and 37% of them regarded it as 'very' useful. There were frequent comments from teachers praising the work of their co-ordinator and saying how useful they found the detailed records of children compiled by the co-ordinator.

The different types and levels of support enjoyed by pupils on the different Stages of the Code of Practice have already been described; the focus of attention now is on the policy and procedures for first recording a child as having special educational needs and subsequently moving him or her between Stages. The majority of the primary schools in the study, 60%, operate their own system of testing for pupils in addition to SATs and any other testing procedures required by the LEA indicating that, as in 1981, there is a high level of testing and assessment activity in primary schools. Standardized reading tests were the most commonly used, but spelling, maths, verbal and non-verbal reasoning tests were also widely used. In exactly half the schools, test results formed part of the basis for first considering that a child should go on to Stage 1 of the Register, but usually test results were only one of the factors considered. Only five schools had a system whereby there was a cut-off point on a test, below which a child would be entered on the Register. Children were most usually placed on the Register because their class teacher felt that there was some cause for concern, though this concern would often be reinforced by poor, or at least unexpectedly low, test scores. The Code of Practice does not require children on Stage 1 to have an Individual Action Plan or to receive any extra provision; it is sufficient that they are monitored. However over 60% of the study schools did make extra provision for pupils on Stage 1, particularly those perceived as having learning difficulties.

Test results become more significant in the decision to move children on to Stage 2; this is at least part of the procedure in 60% of cases, and the number of schools using a cut-off point has risen to nine. However, a child's progress, which may be assessed and recorded in an extremely wide variety of ways, together with the professional opinion of the class teacher, are usually viewed as being of the greatest relevance. Children on Stage 2 have an Individual Action Plan and the development of this plan, its review and updating are usually the responsibility principally of the co-ordinator in collaboration with the class teacher and possibly a member of a support service. However, as with virtually everything else to do with special educational needs, this is not always the case.

In some instances, for example, the class teacher may draw up the Individual Action Plan in collaboration with the Learning Support Service, but the major role is more usually taken by the special educational needs co-ordinator. The co-ordinators in the study had mixed feelings about Individual Action Plans, although nearly all found that they did have their uses. Only one co-ordinator regarded them as not useful at all, arguing that they encouraged all the effort to be put into assessment and recording rather than teaching. Although this was a very minority view expressed in such an extreme form, many other co-ordinators felt that there was some truth in these criticisms. Nearly half of the co-ordinators (46%) were critical of Individual Action Plans even though, overall, they found them useful. The most usual complaint was that the process was very time-consuming, but they were also criticized for taking the emphasis away from actual teaching, for substituting 'writing about it for actually doing it' and for accentuating the 'differentness' of special educational needs children, even when their difficulties were minor and temporary.

It is at Stage 3 that the resource implications of provision become particularly apparent and the variations between LEAs' polices come to have a bigger impact on schools. The level of need associated with Stage 3 is usually accompanied by assistance from at least one of the support services; the level of funding often increases significantly and the level of LEA involvement increases. The use of standardized tests and other assessment procedures required by the LEA, and the use of cut-off points to determine appropriateness of Stage increases substantially. LEAs whose resourcing for special educational needs is based on an audit are able to allocate specific funds to each child who has satisfied predetermined criteria for each Stage, but even LEAs who leave decisions on Stages 1 and 2 to the schools are likely to set their own criteria in relation to Stage 3. The main reason for this is to contain demand. Having pupils on Stage 3 is usually associated with extra resources and, in the absence of any authoritative definition of special educational needs, the Stage at which a pupil is registered is to a certain extent arbitrary. Schools are, therefore, likely to regard it as advantageous to have pupils at Stage 3, in just the same way as heads would like to see more pupils with Statements.

There are sometimes quite elaborate procedures for moving a child from Stage 2 to Stage 3: for instance, a termly special educational needs meeting at the school involving the head, co-ordinator, representatives of the staff and governors, the school's educational psychologist and a senior member of the LEA advisory service, at which the Indivual Education Plans, test results, reports from teachers and all relevant documentation including parental views, are discussed and a decision made on the pupils who can progress to Stage 3. The schools in one authority which had recently moved to this system complained that the whole process was not very different from getting a child Statemented, but the level of extra resources available were very small for the amount of effort involved. Some heads went as far as saying that they thought that it was the intention of the LEA to make the procedures so complicated and time-consuming that schools would not bother and would try to cope from within their existing budgets.

The Code of Practice underlines the importance of parents being involved in the process of entering a child on the special educational needs Register and subsequently being assessed, moved between Stages and having their progress reviewed. Parents are increasingly seen as having an important role to play in the education of their children, and schools are encouraged to seek an active partnership with parents. This sort of close involvement has a longer history in special education than in education more generally (Mittler and Mittler, 1982) and, although the idea of educational professionals and parents working in partnership has frequently been criticized for falling far short of the mark (Armstrong, 1995; Fulcher, 1989), there is, in principle, a consensus on the desirability of parental involvement.

The class teachers in the study schools had seen the parents of 86% of their pupils with special educational needs. (This does not necessarily mean that the parents were unknown to the school in the remaining 14% of cases as they may have seen the head or the co-ordinator without seeing the class teacher.) This figure represents a substantial increase on 1981 when the class teachers had seen the parents of 72.5% of their pupils with special educational needs (Moses and Croll, 1987). When the increase in the number of pupils with special educational needs is also taken into account there appears to be an even bigger increase in the amount of home/school contact about special educational needs issues.

On the whole, teacher/parent contact increases as children move on to higher stages of the Register. Teachers have seen rather under 70% (68.8) of the parents of pupils whom they think have special educational needs but are not on the Register, but over 80% (83.1) of parents whose children are on Stage 1 and over 90% (92.5) of children who have a Statement. They are also more likely to see parents of children on Stages 4 and 5 more often; teachers had seen 60% of the parents of these children four times or more in the current school year, compared with only 6% of children not on the Register. This rough measure of school/parent contact says nothing about the quality of the relationships established, but it does indicate a substantial amount of interaction between teachers and parents.

There are numerous ways of operating the Code of Practice's system of Stages. The following examples give some idea of the diversity of practice but is by no means definitive.

School 1

In this school the procedure for first putting a child on the special educational needs Register is very simple and informal; if the class teacher
feels that a child is giving any cause for concern their parents are
contacted and they go on to Stage 1. At this point their progress is
carefully monitored and recorded but they are not given any extra
help. If the monitoring shows that they are not getting any better, or
if they are actually deteriorating, then further action is taken. The co-
ordinator herself carries out a phonological assessment and gives the
child a standardized reading test chosen by the school. If the child has
a reading age of more than a year behind his or her chronological age,
then further assessment is carried out by a learning support teacher
who is part of the learning support service. This support teacher will
also help the class teacher to draw up an Individual Education Plan,
but though the learning support service is involved in this assessment
it is the school rather than the service which will provide the extra help
for the child. If there is no improvement after a term of help on Stage
2, then the parents are approached for permission for the educational
psychologist to be brought in. Other relevant support services (Behavioural Support, Sensory Impairment, etc.) will also be contacted at this
point and the process to move a child to Stage 3 will not be very
different from assessing a child for a Statement.

School 2

The situation is different in School 2. This school is in an LEA which
requests schools to carry out an extensive annual programme of
testing with all its pupils. NFER Reading, English, Maths and Verbal
Reasoning Tests together with additional spelling tests are used. All
children who score below 85 on any of these tests are automatically
put on the Register at Stage 1. The test results of individual children
are discussed by the class teacher, the co-ordinator and sometimes the
learning support service and a joint decision on the appropriate action
is taken. All the children are monitored and will have differentiated
work and many, in addition, will also have an Individual Education
Plan if school resources allow. On the basis of the same test results it
may be decided, mainly dependent on the professional judgement of
the class teacher, to put a child onto Stage 2. This will ensure that some
sort of 'extra' help is provided. As the learning support service is
already involved in the decisions on Stages 1 and 2, no different
procedure is used for Stage 3, but pupils are more likely to receive
actual teaching help from the support services. This school regards the
LEA's provision for pupils on Stage 3 as relatively generous, but is

keen to stress that it needs to be because it is virtually impossible to get a Statement for a child.

School 3
This school is in a very newly formed Unitary Authority. Staff at the school are unsure exactly what authority-wide procedures are in place but have clear procedures of their own. All children in Key Stage 2 do a standardized reading test twice a year and their performance is regarded as giving 'cause for concern' if they are in Year 3 and their reading age is a year behind their chronological age; if they are in Year 4 with a reading age eighteen months younger than their actual age; and if their reading age is two years or more behind their chronological age if they are in Year 5 or Year 6. The class teacher, in collaboration with the co-ordinator, decide which Stage and how much extra help is appropriate for each child and pupils are moved between Stages on the basis of progress made and reading age. At the time of the research the school had had no contact with the learning support service, which was in the process of being established, so the move from Stage 2 to Stage 3 was much less significant than in most other cases. Nevertheless the school did make it something of a landmark by involving the head in the process. Here it is not until the possibility of assessment for a Statement occurs that the school psychological service is involved.

School 4
The situation in this school is in marked contrast to School 3, principally because School 4 is in an authority which operates the Code of Practice and the allocation of resources on the basis of a special educational needs audit. There is an authority-wide system of testing using NFER Reading and Maths Tests and a special educational needs Audit Manual detailing assessment procedures for all ages and across all special educational needs. This system leaves only a limited amount of discretion to the individual school; for the most part, what they have to do is follow the procedures in the Manual. For Stages 1 and 2 schools follow the procedures on their own, but if they want to move a child to Stage 3 they have to fill in an LEA referral form, showing in detail how the procedures in the special educational needs Audit Manual have been followed and with what result. This is then considered by the school psychological service or another relevant support service and, if considered to be in order, the child can be moved to Stage 3. A similar process, but involving the school psychological service from the start, will move a child onto Stage 5. At

each Stage pupils with particular types of special educational needs will attract predetermined funding, but the exact nature of the provision can vary case by case. This system, on the one hand, creates a lot of paperwork for the special educational needs co-ordinator, but on the other hand the whole procedure and the resource implications are transparent and the same system operates throughout all of this large non-metropolitan authority.

THE SUPPORT SERVICES

As in 1981, all of the study schools were in LEAs who ran a school psychological service and a range of other support services, and all the schools used at least some of these services. Most LEAs substantially increased their support services around the time of the implementation of the 1981 Act in 1983 (Moses *et al.*, 1988). Since that time they have been cut back again and have fluctuated both in size and function (Fletcher-Campbell, 1993; Bangs, 1993). The organization of support services varies substantially between LEAs. It is particularly complex in very newly formed Unitary Authorities which may still have some elements of previous authorities in operation or may have temporary arrangements while new procedures are being developed. By and large the support services will provide assistance to schools to help them meet the needs of their pupils on Stage 3 or higher of the Code of Practice, but practice varies widely. Here the work of the support services will be considered only from the school's perspective and will deal with the amount of contact between the services and the schools, what type of service they provide, whether schools are satisfied with the support they are getting and whether they would like more of it.

In the interviews, headteachers, class teachers and special educational needs co-ordinators were all asked about their contacts with various support services. For each they were asked about the extent of contact, the kind of work the service did, how satisfied they were with the service, and whether they would like more of this kind of provision. From these data, which is presented in Table 7.3, it would appear that it is generally the heads and the co-ordinators rather than class teachers who directly deal with the support services, though they may well be indirectly affected through the assessment of individual children and the advice given to the co-ordinator.

Table 7.3: Teachers, heads, special educational needs co-ordinators and the support services

		Type of contact					Satisfaction			
		Total contact %	Regular contact %	Assessment %	Work with children %	Assessment and work with children %	Yes %	No %	Mixed %	More contact %
SPS	Head	45 93.8	80.0	77.8	0	22.2	46.7	28.9	24.4	82.2
	SENCO	44 97.8	59.1	86.4	2.3	11.4	52.3	25.0	22.7	84.1
	Teacher	116 38.8	32.8	87.1	2.6	10.3	54.3	32.8	12.1	71.6
Learning support	Head	32 66.7	100.0	28.1	6.3	65.6	75.0	18.8	6.3	78.1
	SENCO	36 80.0	86.1	38.9	0	61.1	72.2	22.2	5.6	80.6
	Teacher	110 36.8	80.0	23.6	30.0	45.5	77.3	15.5	6.4	81.8
EBD	Head	27 56.3	66.7	14.8	7.4	74.1	55.6	29.6	11.1	63.0
	SENCO	24 53.3	66.7	16.7	25.0	50.0	58.3	20.8	20.8	70.8
	Teacher	26 8.7	50.0	23.1	34.6	38.5	38.5	30.8	30.8	65.4
Sensory impairment	Head	25 52.1	48.0	28.0	20.0	52.0	88.0	4.0	8.0	36.0
	SENCO	19 42.2	52.6	47.4	15.8	36.8	100.0	0	0	15.8
	Teacher	12 4.0	75.0	25.0	16.7	58.3	91.7	8.3	0	33.3
Speech therapy	Head	27 56.3	40.7	11.1	7.4	70.4	48.2	29.6	14.8	63.0
	SENCO	26 57.8	42.3	23.1	0	76.9	61.5	23.1	15.4	73.1
	Teacher	28 9.4	25.0	46.4	10.7	42.9	67.9	25.0	7.1	42.9
Medical services	Head	45 93.8	64.4	26.7	8.9	64.4	95.6	4.4	0	33.3
	SENCO	22 48.9	54.5	31.8	13.6	54.5	95.5	4.5	0	27.5
	Teacher	69 23.1	34.8	46.1	14.5	39.1	85.5	11.6	2.9	27.5

The School Psychological Service

There were only three schools, all of them very small schools, who had not been in contact with the school psychological service during the current school year. Most contact was made by the heads and the co-ordinators, although only heads were likely to have regular contact. In contrast, under 40% of class teachers had any direct contact, and this was mostly of an occasional nature. This does not mean that they were not in some way helped by the educational psychologist's work in the school, but it does indicate that any such help is indirect. This pattern of contact is in fact much the same as in 1981 when all contact between schools and the school psychological service went through the head and a third of class teachers personally saw their educational psychologist to discuss individual children. The vast majority of the work of the school psychological service in schools is concerned with assessment, and many schools only see them in this context; but there is a small amount of work carried out directly with children.

There were mixed reactions to the support provided by the school psychological service; only about a half of all the heads, special educational needs co-ordinators and class teachers with recent direct experience of the service said that they were satisfied with the help they were getting. However, the fact that over 80% of the heads and co-ordinators and over 70% of the class teachers wanted to see more of their educational psychologist suggests that they are, on the whole, dissatisfied with the quantity rather than the quality of the help they are getting. Several headteachers talked about problems with the shortage of educational psychologist time available; one head put it like this: 'school psychological service support is both well intentioned and expert but there is simply not enough of it. We don't know if this really is the case but it appears that the educational psychologists have been briefed to reduce the number of Statements, but there is never enough time or opportunities to discuss this and possible alternative strategies.' Another complained that their educational psychologist only ever had time to administer tests to children when the teachers would have liked her to observe children in the classroom as well. The educational psychologist too said that she would prefer to do this but there was just not enough time. Despite the shortage of time available, several heads were anxious to emphasize the professional commitment of their educational psychologists who 'were always available to talk about any child over the phone' and who 'has been absolutely invaluable liaising with families that we had found it very difficult to deal with.' There were several mentions of how valuable INSET courses run by the school psychological service had been, but unfortunately the following comment is more typical: 'They could offer training and advice to staff and I'm sure it would be worthwhile but the school cannot take it up. We are allowed five sessions of educational psychologist time a year and it is entirely taken up with pupil assessments.'

As one of the earlier comments made clear, schools are very conscious of the 'gatekeeping' role of the school psychological service. This is most apparent in relation to Statements, but in many instances they also control access to the other support services so no child can move on to Stage 3 and become eligible for help from, for example, the Behavioural Support Team without recommendation from an educational psychologist. When the school psychological service have to take on this function, time for work other than assessments is stretched even further. As one head put it, 'Now that an educational psychologist has to be involved in every decision that a child should move from Stage 2 to Stage 3 there is an impossible bottleneck and everyone involved is overstretched to the point that they cannot do their job properly.'

There were a number of interesting comments that illustrate that, although it may be the structure and operation of the system that will in the end determine the quality and the quantity of the service, schools were very aware that the personal qualities of their particular educational psychologist made a lot of difference. Comments ranged from 'We find that personal commitment is lacking. The school doesn't get its allocation. We would like some regular commitment instead of having to constantly chase the educational psychologist to try to get a slot in his diary. It isn't very satisfactory' to 'We are not at all satisfied with the system but our particular educational psychologist is absolutely brilliant. We couldn't hope for more.'

Other Support Services
Nearly all the schools in the study had recently seen at least one of the medical services; only three small schools had not had any such contact. For the purpose of this overview of services, all the various medical services are considered together though they in fact cover a wide range of types of provision ranging from the school nurse who will see all or most children to physiotherapists who will work with a very small number of individual children. Services are mostly involved in both assessment and work with individual children, though a small number will only do one or the other. Most of the schools' contact with the medical services is with the head; only half the special educational needs co-ordinators and fewer than a quarter

of class teachers have seen any of them recently. There is a very high level of satisfaction with these services, and most schools feel that they do not need to see more of them.

Far fewer schools reported any recent contact with services for the hearing or visually impaired. Just over half of the heads and 40% of the co-ordinators had been in contact with staff from these services, and only 4% of teachers. There was, however, a very high level of satisfaction with the work of these services expressed by nearly all who had recent experience of contact and, for the most part, schools felt that the quantity as well as the quality of service that they received was satisfactory.

The situation in relation to speech therapy and speech and language services was rather more varied. Rather more than half the head teachers and co-ordinators and one in ten class teachers had contact with this service, but it tended to be occasional rather than regular. As with the more specialist of the medical services, children do not necessarily receive help from these services at school but may attend outside clinics. The work of most services is seen by schools to involve both assessment and work with children, but teachers are more inclined than heads and co-ordinators to feel that they concentrate mainly on assessment. On the other hand, class teachers are more likely to be satisfied with the service and to consider that they receive enough help.

The highest level of contact was between primary schools and learning support services; all the schools in the study, even the smallest, had regular contact between, at least, the head and the learning support service. It has already been established that learning difficulties dominate special educational needs in the primary classroom, so the universal use of these services is not surprising. About two-thirds of the schools reported that their learning support service both assessed children and worked directly with them. There has been a general shift in the work of learning and other support services since the early 1980s, away from the direct teaching of children to the giving of advice and the carrying out of assessments (Fletcher-Campbell, 1993). There is however still a considerable amount of work done directly with children, and interestingly far more class teachers see this as being the main activity of the learning support service.

There was a tendency for schools to have definite views about the work of this service. Heads, co-ordinators and class teachers all expressed a high level of satisfaction with the service with about three-quarters saying that they were pleased with the quality of support they were getting, and under 20% being dissatisfied; only 6% had mixed feelings. There was little difference between the views of heads, co-ordinators and class teachers, but it was the class teachers who were most likely to be satisfied. Schools clearly appreciate the help given by their learning support service and they also want more of it; 80% of the schools would like to see more of their learning support service.

The second most frequently perceived special educational need is emotional and behavioural difficulties, but the study schools received proportionately far less help in this area from support services. Just over half of the heads and co-ordinators, but under 10% of class teachers, had dealings with a behaviour support service. When the numbers of children whom teachers regard as having emotional and behavioural difficulties are considered, then the level of support appears to be low. At the time of the first study, none of the schools were in authorities that ran a specialist support service, though schools did receive help in this area from the school psychological service. From the early 1980s an increasing number of specialist services have been established and the recent government directive to all LEAs to draw up plans to address the problems of both emotional and behavioural difficulties and exclusion are increasing activity in this area. It is relevant here to remember that although these problems are seen to be very prevalent, teachers are not always anxious for more help to be provided.

There were mixed reactions to the help that the behaviour support service provided; overall rather over half of the heads and the co-ordinators were satisfied, but under 40% of class teachers shared this view, which represented the lowest level of satisfaction with any of the support services. At least to some extent, this dissatisfaction was connected with not getting enough help, as nearly two-thirds of the teachers who used the service wanted more help from the behaviour support service.

PREVENTION

There was no consensus of opinion among heads and special educational needs co-ordinators about the part that schools may possibly play in the prevention of special educational needs. The question, 'Do you think that schools can play a major role in preventing special educational needs arising?' has already been discussed in Chapter 5. As we saw there, it elicited a very wide variety of responses ranging from, 'No. Of course we can't stop special educational needs arising. I wish we could. All we can do is to respond as effectively as possible' to 'Oh yes. We can do a lot. What else are schools for?' Altogether nine heads, rather under 20%, felt that schools could not actually prevent special educational needs from arising, while 28 (nearly 60%) thought that schools could do a lot in the way of prevention, and the rest were of the opinion that they could make some difference in some cases. The position of the co-ordinators was rather different; they were, on the whole, rather less optimistic, with about a third thinking that schools could play a major preventative role and half thinking that schools could perhaps prevent the occurrence of some special educational needs.

These differences are difficult to explain; but some, at least partial, explanations can be suggested. It has already been established that there is a strong tendency for class teachers to see the aetiology of special educational needs as lying outside the school and therefore beyond their control. It is also the case that some of the heads themselves tend to explain changes in the incidence of special educational needs in terms of catchment areas and similar factors. If the origins of special educational needs are seen as lying outside the school, then a belief that schools can only play a limited role in prevention is likely to follow. Nevertheless many heads and co-ordinators do in fact see a role for schools in this area.

A wide range of strategies were mentioned; some specifically targeted on special educational needs and others of a more general nature. There were school behaviour policies aimed at creating a good atmosphere in which all children are less likely to behave in a problematic fashion. Some heads claimed that, at least in part, the remedy was simple and that 'good teaching', especially the good teaching of reading, would prevent learning difficulties from arising. These approaches can be regarded as being genuinely aimed at prevention and include all pupils but many others are rather different. Thirty-seven of the heads (77%) and 28 of the co-ordinators (60%) spoke of the value of early intervention for the 'prevention' of special educational needs . It is debatable whether strategies for early intervention can accurately be viewed in this way, though that is not to be critical of them in any way. In early intervention strategies, individual children are targeted as requiring 'special' help because they have already given some indication that they have a greater need than other children; that is, they have special educational needs. Nevertheless, if difficulties are identified early it may be possible to prevent them from developing into anything more serious. Although there are conceptual differences between genuine prevention and early intervention, and in some instances the two sorts of practice will be readily distinguishable, that will not always be the case and sometimes prevention and early intervention appear to merge.

There were many examples of initiatives taken by schools to attempt to reduce the incidence of special educational needs. For instance one school was keen to emphasize its work with parents, especially the 'Pre-school Advice Partnership' run for the parents of prospective pupils which offered parents advice on pre-reading, reading and number games that they could use at home with their small children to prepare them for school. Another school had introduced the complete 'Reading Recovery' scheme and had found it very successful. Several schools mentioned a policy of concentrating on children on Stage 1 with the idea that extra effort put in early could stop their difficulties from escalating. Another popular strategy was to concentrate attention on the youngest children in the school, whether these children were in the nursery, the reception class or in the first class in the junior school (Year 3), again with the idea of picking up problems as early as possible.

It must be borne in mind that at the same time that these initiatives are being put into action the numbers of primary schoolchildren perceived as having special educational needs is actually rising. Perhaps the combination of the emphasis on special educational needs, the individualization of difficulties underlined by the Code of Practice and particularly Individual Education Plans, and the well-established idea that a large number of children have special educational needs, predisposes schools to become increasingly sensitive to individual differences and to regard an increasing number of these difficulties as constituting special educational needs.

—8———————————————

The local education authority and special educational needs

This study, like its predecessor in 1981, is principally concerned with children, teachers and schools rather than with LEAs, but schools operate within the context of local education authorities whose policy and provision impact on schools. The sample of schools used is large, and chosen so that it represents a national picture. However, there are insufficient schools in each LEA to enable us to say with any confidence how different LEA policy, in relation to special educational needs provision, affects what happens in schools. It was not possible to do this in 1981 when our schools were spread over ten LEAs; now, because of the establishment of Unitary Authorities, the study involves fifteen LEAs, sometimes with only one study school. Nevertheless it is important to consider the role played by LEAs in the provision of education for children with special educational needs.

The changes in legislation affecting special educational needs provision have already been mentioned. Since 1944 there have been three major pieces of legislation affecting special education and other Education Acts that, although not dealing specifically with special educational needs, nevertheless have made a major impact. As the main implementers of legislation, the LEAs are directly affected by educational law. It could be argued that, especially in terms of human rights, the most significant Act was the 1970 Education Act which declared that no child should be regarded as uneducable and consequently the responsibility for the provision of education for *all* children should rest with the LEA. Previously provision for the most seriously handicapped children was the responsibility of the National Health Service and, although they might have provided education of a sort, the emphasis was quite definitely on care. The inclusion of all children within the same education system was a very major landmark in educational and social policy. The children previously cared for by the National Health Service may not have been included with their neighbourhood mainstream school but they were brought into the education system. The 1970 legislation had a major impact on LEAs as they were made responsible for more children who required a new type of provision. The numbers involved may have been relatively small, approximately 24,000 children, but the provision required was complex and the principle involved was profound.

Much has been written about the 1981 Act and we shall not pursue a detailed account here, but it is worthwhile outlining the most salient points. The three most important aspects of this legislation abandoned the system of categorizing individuals according to handicap, introducing the term 'special educational needs' with the intention that it should have a much wider application; established the principle that children should be educated together in the same classrooms but with conditions that rendered this position relatively weak; and introduced the 'Statementing' procedure.

At the time, the 1981 Act was generally welcomed. The Warnock Report which had preceded it in 1978 was enthusiastically received and the consensus of opinion was pleased to see most of Warnock's key recommendations enshrined in law. Goacher *et al.* (1988) found that in 1983 LEAs were enthusiastic about the possibilities for provision that the implementation of the Act offered, but were keen to emphasize the fact that this position was the direct result of both the consultation that took place between central and local government and, connected with this, the fact that the new law, for the most part, formalized what was already generally regarded as good practice.

Moses *et al.* (1988) found that many LEAs had instituted policy changes in response to Warnock, regarding this as the right direction in which to go, whether or not it was later backed up by force of law. This applies to the acceptance of the term special educational needs which appears to have found almost universal favour at the time, together with the principle of integration. A statement supporting the principle of integration was contained in most LEA policy documents well before the implementation of the 1981 Act in April 1993. The introduction of Statementing was a different matter altogether. Although it was not met with the degree of hostility that might have been expected, it is unlikely that any LEA would have devised and implemented this system had it not been a legal requirement.

Similarly the 1993 Act and the subsequent Code of Practice in 1994 were broadly welcomed for the same reasons. Millward and Skidmore provide detailed accounts of the positive reactions to this legislation by LEA officers and members who were particularly impressed by the level of consultation that they were involved in with central government (Millward and Skidmore, 1995). The 1993 Act did not fundamentally change the key elements of the 1981 legislation but put time limits on assessment procedures, made other minor procedural changes and gave increased powers to parents, especially through the establishment of the Special Educational Needs Tribunal (Harries, 1997), through which parents can challenge the decisions of the LEA.

The Act does, however, have a real significance for LEAs because it identifies the key role that they are to play in special educational needs education. They have direct statutory responsibility for all pupils with Statements and there is a requirement for them to collaborate with special and mainstream schools in the implementation of the Code of Practice, to provide special support for pupils at Stage 3, and also to ensure the maintenance of provision for minority groups within the special educational needs population. Additionally LEAs have the responsibility for improving the overall efficiency of their management of resources within special education.

When the 1981 Act was implemented in April 1983 the role of the LEAs in implementation was clear. Ten years later the situation was very different. The 1988 Education Reform Act seriously reduced the authority of the LEA over schools; some schools opted for the newly created Grant Maintained Status which put them outside the authority of the LEA, but all schools were affected by the introduction of Local Management of Schools (LMS) schemes which obliged LEAs to delegate the vast majority of schools' budgets to the schools themselves, thus seriously undermining the traditional role of the LEA to the point where there was some question over whether they did in fact have a future. In this context the 1983 Act can be seen as re-establishing the LEA, even if in a rather reduced and modified role. Providing special educational needs education is now central to what LEAs do, forming a much larger proportion of their total activity than had traditionally been the case. They are directly responsible for the education of pupils with Statements and responsible, with schools, for provision for non-Statemented special educational needs. There is some blurring of lines of responsibility in relation to non-Statemented special educational needs between schools and the LEA which are frequently a major cause of contention.

There has been considerable legislative activity in education in general and special educational needs in particular since data for the original *One in Five* study was collected but the extent to which policy and particularly provision has actually changed is much more problematic. It does appear to be the case that many of the issues and concerns that were apparent in 1981 are still, or again, issues now.

CHANGES IN THE LEAS

In 1998 when data for the project was being gathered from schools and
LEAs, many local authorities were experiencing a period of change
and transition. The establishment of the new Unitary Authorities has
created problems for special educational needs provision and the
Local Government Review which preceded it also caused some difficulties for authorities who, in the end, have not been affected because
of the uncertainty involved. It appears that the effects of at least some
aspects of this type of change are immediate. They can also be very
long-lasting. For instance, some large non-metropolitan authorities
with very diverse types of special educational needs provision in
different areas of the authority still attribute these differences to variations that existed prior to the reorganization of local government in
1974. These differences are particularly apparent in the provision of
special schools. LEAs have always varied considerably in the number
and type of special schools they have run and the proportion of the
school-age population attending them. A boundary change that
results in an LEA either acquiring new special schools or losing them
is likely to have a major impact on the LEAs affected. When the ILEA
was disbanded and the inner London education authorities were
established in 1989–90 the new authorities found that they had very
varied numbers of special schools within their boundaries, as the
previous provision of ILEA had not been geographically evenly
spread. The variation was such that one small authority had seven
special schools while an adjoining authority had none at all. These
problems are now being experienced by most, if not all, of the LEAs
affected by the recent creation of unitary authorities. These new
authorities tend to be small in size and this in itself can create
problems. To develop policy and organize and deliver high quality
education across the whole of the diverse special educational needs
population requires wide-ranging expertise, and the number of
appointments required to cover all areas may be difficult for a very
small authority to achieve. There is of course no reason why small
authorities should not work together in collaboration to provide some
services, particularly those catering for low incidence needs, and it is
the declared intention of some small Unitary Authorities to do this.
Nevertheless there is a long history of LEAs seeking, as far as possible,
to provide for all the children and young people within their boundaries, and some LEAs within our study are currently reporting
problems created in this way. For instance the division of a previously
large non-metropolitan authority into two parts, in effect the county

town and the rest of the county, has resulted in a disproportionate division of some forms of special educational needs provision. The officers responsible for special educational needs in the 'county' authority report that the new 'city' authority has inherited the largest and the best part of the old authority's Pupil Referral Units, of which the new authority has exclusive use. This has left the 'county' short of such provision, while at the same time the 'city' are not using some of the 'county' special schools, leaving these schools with suddenly seriously depleted roles and an uncertain future. Even the loss of one individual in a key role during reorganization can cause uncertainty in establishing the policy of a new authority, and is particularly likely to cause delays in implementation. Some of these difficulties will be short-term and solvable, but the effects of others are likely to have repercussions for years to come.

There are insufficient schools in any one authority in this study for us to be certain about the exact effects of particular types of LEA policy on provision in schools. However, it is clear that the uncertainty caused by reorganization, and felt so acutely in the Education Office, also manifests itself to schools. In spite of the plethora of 'reforms' and new initiatives with which primary schools have been concerned over the last few years, special educational needs is still a major concern. It is also one of the areas of activity where schools are most directly affected by LEA policy and practice. At a time of generally decreasing local authority power, LEAs still exercise considerable discretion over all aspects of special educational needs provision, from the running of special schools to the allocation of resources to mainstream schools for special educational needs, the operation of the Code of Practice, the running of support services and the creation and maintenance of the organizational framework within which special educational needs education, whatever its location or type, is provided. From the perspective of mainstream primary schools it is the allocation of resources for special educational needs which is the key issue.

SPECIAL SCHOOLS

The subject of this particular study is special educational needs in the mainstream primary school, and it is not possible to broaden this focus of attention in any detail. Nevertheless it needs to be borne in mind that provision in mainstream schools is closely connected to LEA policy on special schools as well. This point is clearly made in a 1999 policy document of one of the participating authorities: 'it is recognised that any decision about special school provision needs also to take account of the pattern of provision in mainstream schools with enhanced resources for special educational needs and student support centres, as well as policies covering the organisation of mainstream schools'. Since the early 1980s LEA policy documents have contained a statement of commitment first to 'integration' and currently to 'inclusion'. There has been an overall reduction in the number of special schools, and LEAs have varied greatly in the moves they have made towards full inclusion. However, overall, the outstanding characteristic of the special school sector has been its resilience (Croll and Moses, 1999). In this context the most relevant factors are the commitment, on the LEAs' part, to moving towards inclusion on the one hand, which directly affects mainstream schools by at least potentially widening the range of children who may attend them, while at the same time maintaining special schools to cater for pupils whom mainstream schools are unable or reluctant to accept. At the same time as making a commitment to the principle of inclusion, LEAs maintain special schools while acknowledging the problem this creates.

One of the LEAs in our study wanted to move to inclusive provision but at the same time was actually experiencing an increase in the number of pupils in its special schools, even though they acknowledged that 'the creation of more special-school places is likely to lead to their being filled'. Although the origins for this situation are complex the main underlying reason is contained in the second half of the sentence, 'but it is considered important to make appropriate school provision, in order to meet, as far as possible, the needs of *all* the authority's children within the county'. We demonstrate elsewhere that an emphasis on each individual child and parent within the present system is associated with small-scale, or incremental change, which is unlikely to result in any major change towards increased inclusion (Croll and Moses, 1999). Despite the commitment in principle to inclusion on the part of LEAs and most of the education establishment, special schools are often popular with both parents and mainstream schools. One of the consequences of the continued provision of special schools is the attitude that they encourage in many mainstream schools; that a whole specialist sector of education exists to deal with 'difficult' children so they do not have to. This may be an excessively blunt way of expressing this position, but without doubt it is relevant to the thinking of many mainstream schools.

There has for a number of years now been a notion that close contact between mainstream and special schools could be advantageous. The most recent official expression of this position was contained in the 1997 Green Paper, *Excellence for All Children – Meeting Special Educational Needs,* which suggests closer collaboration between special schools, support services and mainstream schools. This possible development is, it appears, seen mainly from a special school perspective. The Paper says:

> *In all this there are exciting opportunities for special schools.* [our italics] Increasingly, they will be providing a varied pattern of support for children with special educational needs. Some children will be full-time placements, others part-time or short-term; staff will be supporting some children in mainstream placements; they will be helping mainstream schools to implement inclusion policies; and they will be a source of training and advice for mainstream colleagues. It may be that when the role has developed to this extent, the term 'special school' will be seen as an inadequate reflection of what they do. (Department for Education and Employment, 1997, p. 51)

At least on the face of it this proposal appears to have much to recommend it, but it is salutary to remember that this area, together with several other issues and concerns that have been presented as 'new' and 'innovative' in the field of special educational needs in the 1990s, actually had their origins a considerable time ago. Similar ideas were expounded in the Warnock Report, where many current ideas about special educational needs and provision are to be found, in 1978. A number of LEAs and indeed some special and mainstream schools with only minimal involvement from the authority, operated a wide variety of linked schemes involving movement of both staff and pupils between mainstream and special schools and, in a small number of cases, this led to the absorption of the special school by the mainstream school. A study of these schemes, *Joining Forces* (Jowett *et al.,* 1988), reported the extensive involvement of special schools in 'linked' schemes, some of which had at that time been in operation for several years. In a follow-up study Fletcher-Campbell found a reduced number of such schemes still in operation (Fletcher-Campbell, 1993).

There are a number of points to be made here. First, widening the role of the special school may be a way of 'saving' special schools (and it is of course debatable to what extent that is a desirable thing) but there are insufficient special schools to think of them as the main source of special educational needs support for mainstream schools.

Of the 48 schools in the present study only eleven were involved in any sort of link scheme, none of a very substantial nature. Even in an LEA where all schools were members of a 'family' of schools which included special schools, the contacts were not extensive.

As with other aspects of special educational needs provision (which will be considered later) LMS had an impact on linked schemes. Until the introduction of LMS, schools could relatively easily make arrangements for pupils to spend time in other schools, or for teachers to work partly in other schools. Provided that the LEA approved of the use of its resources, the schemes could proceed on a relatively informal basis without having to be concerned about exactly which school's budget paid for what. LMS put an end to that; it did not prevent linked schemes of a variety of sorts being continued, and indeed being established, but it did necessitate very careful financial planning, and many schemes ceased to operate. Jowett *et al.* describe various types of relationship that could operate between LEAs and schools in this respect and suggest that those where the LEA is closely involved are likely to be the most enduring; under the current financial arrangements these are the only schemes that have any viability (Jowett *et al.*, 1988).

The Green Paper is now suggesting such schemes as a major innovation at the time when one of the LEAs in our study is considering whether or not to initiate such a scheme for the second time around. This authority, following up the suggestion in the Warnock Report for a new role for special schools, created a support service operated from three special schools staffed by special-school teachers to provide help for mainstream primary schools. Despite the best of intentions, the scheme was not a success. Considerable dissatisfaction with the quality and reliability of support offered was expressed by the mainstream schools while, at the same time, it appeared that at least some of the special-school staff were actively involved in a recruitment drive for their own special schools. Although there may be advantages to be gained from close contacts between special and mainstream schools, there are, without a doubt, pitfalls.

SOME FUNDING ISSUES

Provision for special educational needs is expensive, and it is not clear either how large the total special educational needs population is nor how to judge when these needs are actually being met. At a time when there is considerable emphasis on resource allocation and 'value for money' it is not surprising that LEAs are concerned about special educational needs spending. The following extreme expression of concern appeared in the policy statement of a metropolitan authority in 1999: 'The cost of providing for children with special educational needs has risen steeply in recent years, and, if present trends continue unchecked, it is considered that the LEA's statutory duties for children with special educational needs could overwhelm other important priorities.'

Whether the situation is actually more difficult now, or is perceived as being more acute because of the emphasis on 'value for money', coupled with the increased centrality of the role of special educational needs provision, is difficult to say; there has always been pressure on the special educational needs budget. Although it is a near-impossible task to accurately cost and compare the financial implications of special school and mainstream plus support provision, there is no doubt that special schooling is expensive. In a move that is perhaps unusual in the education service, many LEAs have attempted to transfer funding from special schools to mainstream, thus pursuing the principled objective of inclusion while holding spending in check; being able to pursue principle and economy is a welcome change. In a study of support offered to mainstream schools, Moses *et al.* (1988) analyse the adjustments made to a special education budget as part of the implementation of the 1981 Act. The emphasis in this instance lay in reducing the numbers of pupils who were placed in special provision for the hearing-impaired in schools outside the authority. At this time, in the early 1980s, there was the wish on the part of LEAs to achieve economies, but also a desire to make proper educational provision for these children inside the authority and closer to their homes and, wherever possible, in mainstream schools. To this end 'out county' placements were reduced as far as was compatible with parental wishes, and the funds thus saved were used to establish a support service for children with hearing impairment and their teachers in mainstream schools; it was also possible to establish a new post of Adviser for special educational needs. In this way, the reallocation of funds had a substantial and lasting impact on the type of provision offered.

LEAs are still in the process of trying to proceed in this way; in principle it may seem straightforward, but in practice it can be fraught with difficulty. A large metropolitan authority in our study is currently attempting to reallocate funds from special-school provision to resourced provision in mainstream schools plus a support service. This authority has been committed first to 'integration' then to 'inclusion' for a number of years and, in some areas, this policy has been successfully pursued. Nevertheless, special schools catering for pupils with moderate learning difficulties have proved very resistant to change. At the moment it is this area of provision that has been targeted for change. In outline, the plan is to reduce the number of special schools for pupils with moderate learning difficulties, to sell these sites as they will be surplus to authority requirements, and to use the substantial sums of money released to establish a support service that will support pupils with moderate learning difficulties and their teachers in mainstream schools. There is no other source of funds available for the establishment of this learning support service, so it is wholly dependent on achieving the closure of the special schools. Although substantial numbers of special schools have been closed during the 1980s and 1990s, it is often a very difficult business.

In this instance the LEA, particularly the senior officers involved, have wanted to reduce the number of moderate learning difficulties special schools for many years, but any plan to do so met with ferocious opposition from the schools themselves; from mainstream schools but particularly from parents. Many parents were strongly supportive of the special schools and were very anxious that their children should not be moved into mainstream schools. The parents were able to secure the support of local councillors who intervened to prevent the officers' plans coming to fruition. This situation has been repeated many times over the years in LEAs all over the country. Despite the weight of educational opinion in favour of inclusion, special schools frequently continue to enjoy the active support of many parents. It is parents, as constituents, who are most likely to be able to exert influence on elected members, and although it may often appear as if it is the officers who exert the most influence, if there is any substantial difference in opinion between officers and members, it is the members whose views carry the most weight.

In the face of this sort of opposition, moves towards closure have been difficult but, over a period of time, the rearrangement of the age phases of the special schools, together with fewer pupils being assessed as needing special-school placements for moderate learning difficulties, has so seriously reduced the school rolls that they are on the point of being educationally unviable. Now there is decreased opposition to the closure of some of the schools and they are likely to proceed. It is interesting to note that, although some schools will close and the support service will be established, the direction that future provision will take is not guaranteed. The senior officers hope that the formation of the support service will provide support for mainstream schools such that the demand for special-school places is reduced, or preferably eliminated. Although this may be achieved, there are many difficulties. A number of special schools will still remain and these will, to some extent, be given a new lease of life through gaining new pupils as other schools close, bringing them to closer to capacity and viability. As has been argued earlier, there is a strong tendency for available special-school places to be filled unless very positive action is taken to resist it.

MAINSTREAM SCHOOLS AND RESOURCE ALLOCATION

Until the 1981 Act the mainstream and special-school sectors of education were mostly run as two separate entities by LEAs, with the local authority exercising real control over both. It was unusual for the two sectors to have contact with each other, though many children, especially those with moderate learning difficulties and behavioural and emotional problems, attended mainstream primary schools before moving to special schools. There were also some children with difficulties from the whole range of special educational needs who spent the whole of their educational careers in ordinary schools; but the system was such that they were not recorded in any way. We do not know how many such children there were, but we do know from the first *One in Five* study that many primary schoolteachers claimed to have experience of teaching children for whom a special-school place would have been a realistic alternative. The 1981 Act did not unite the two sectors, but the combination of extending the meaning of the term special educational needs to cover the whole spectrum of difficulties at all degrees of severity, plus the movement towards increased integration, meant that special education was, without a doubt, the concern of mainstream schools.

Right from the start of the process of implementing the 1981 Act, the issue of resources has dominated the relationship between LEAs and schools. It is inevitable that when need and resources are so closely connected, resource allocation becomes crucial. Of particular significance is the notion of 'extra' provision as an aspect of the definition of special educational needs, especially when this is applied in a climate of financial stringency. It is significant that both the Acts of 1981 and 1993 were regarded by the legislators as financially neutral, while the consensus of informal, professional opinion tended to the conclusion that the financial implications were significant. In the *One in Five* schools in 1981 many of the headteachers felt that cutbacks in LEA expenditure meant that they were worried about maintaining the level of support they were currently offering to pupils with special educational needs. It was in this climate of economic cutback and uncertainty that schools were asked to address the issue of special educational needs legislation.

There was virtually complete agreement with the recommendations of Warnock on the desirability of abandoning the term 'handicap' and the introduction of the term 'special educational needs'. Warnock states: 'To describe someone as handicapped conveys nothing of the type of educational help and hence provision that is required' (Department of Education and Science, 1978, 3:6). In abandoning the terminology of 'handicap' and its lack of reference to provision, Warnock instead brought together 'needs' and 'provision' and defined one in terms of the other, so that the child with special educational needs was the child *who needed special provision*. There was no retracting from this position; from that point onward, needs and provision were inextricably linked. Circular 8/81 (Department of Education and Science, 1981b) which followed the Act clearly accepts the Warnock definition of special educational provision as encompassing 'the whole range and variety of *additional* help, whether it is provided on a full- or part-time basis, by which children may be helped to overcome educational difficulties, however they are caused' (Department of Education and Science, 1978, 3:38). Here, need is defined in terms of provision that is additional or extra to what is generally available, without any consideration of either more independent definitions of need or any notion of 'general availability'. This opens the way for a limitless number of children to demand an infinite amount of extra provision. In retrospect this appears to be a recipe for disaster. Subsequent legislation has not basically changed this position, and the whole issue of resourcing special educational needs provision is still fraught with problems and it is difficult to see any real resolution under the present system.

It is not really surprising that there was a demand for additional resources from schools. In the early 1980s, due to a misunderstanding of the LEA's policy on the implementation of the 1981 Act, a group of secondary headteachers in a large non-metropolitan authority decided that an appropriate action for them to take was to get 'the 20% with SEN' Statemented to attract substantial additional funding. Of course this strategy did not work but, nevertheless, the pressure put on the authority to issue Statements did result in the LEA Statementing a large number of pupils, and a 'culture' of high Statementing was established which the LEA is still struggling to reduce.

The 1988 Education Reform Act had very little to say directly about special educational needs but nevertheless was very relevant to special educational needs provision. Two aspects of the legislation in particular were of significance, both connected with the idea of 'putting education in the marketplace': first, the establishment of league tables where schools' achievements were put on public display, and second, the introduction of LMS which gave schools much more freedom from the LEA over the control of their budgets. In the context of LEA policy on special educational needs it is LMS that is of most significance. Even before the introduction of LMS, at a time when a small number of LEAs were experimenting with greater budgetary control for schools, fears were expressed about the possible consequences (Moses *et al.*, 1988). Particularly when there might be 'higher prestige' options on which to concentrate, it may be tempting for schools to concentrate on these rather than on special educational needs provision. This fear is accentuated by the fact that in this area of provision, unlike any other, the LEA is directly as well as indirectly involved. There is often an indistinct line between services provided from the school's own delegated budget and services that are additionally resourced by the LEA.

The original problem of 'extra' provision is just as, if not more, acute under LMS as it was before. It would hardly be an exaggeration to say that there are as many systems for resource allocation for special educational needs as there are LEAs. The complexity and diversity of LEA resource allocation is well illustrated by Fletcher-Campbell (1996), and in the current research we found arrangements so varied that we had to obtain information from each one with a unique set of questions because of the wide range of options available to LEAs in this matter. It could be argued that some form of standardization might be more desirable, but it would be necessary to establish what constituted 'best practice' and whether the same method could be applied to all LEAs or whether there were variations in relation to size and possibly other characteristics; there is certainly no obviously superior method of proceeding. In principle, to establish the most efficient method is possible but in practice the task is overwhelming. LEAs do not work in total isolation from each other and they do modify practice in the light of knowledge of practices elsewhere; but into the foreseeable future policy and practice will continue to be very varied. This research project has not focused attention on the LEA and will not present detailed accounts of the resource allocation mechanisms, but there are important issues that need consideration here, at least in outline.

STATEMENTS

The process of Statementing was introduced by the 1981 Act. Unlike the previous system of 'ascertainment' for special education which was only applied to pupils who were to attend special schools, the Statement is issued on the basis of need rather than placement. All pupils in special schools are the subjects of Statement, as are an ill-defined additional group of pupils in mainstream schools. The original intention of this arrangement, recommended in the Warnock Report, was as an aid and encouragement to integration; to act as a guarantee that a child or young person with significant special educational needs should receive adequate provision irrespective of the type of school they attended. It was envisaged that Statements would be written for approximately 2% of the school-age population, the figure attending special schools at the time; but because of the lack of clarity about what exactly constitutes special educational needs, and particularly because of the definition of need in terms of 'extra' provision, there has always been a tendency for schools to push for Statements for children who would never be considered for special-school placements, in order to receive additional resources. Since the system began, most LEAs have seen the number of Statements increase and most regard this increase as highly problematic. The number and proportion of pupils with Statements in mainstream schools is not an indication of commitment to integration or inclusion but rather an indication of an aspect of resource allocation. The budgetary implications of the number of Statements is enormous and is of great concern to LEAs. The Coopers and Lybrand report for the Special Educational Needs Initiative (a consortium of LEAs) emphasizes the significance of Statements and points out two factors with serious consequences that are often overlooked. First, once a Statement has been written for a child, despite annual reviews, it is rarely withdrawn but lasts the length of the child's education; and second, as part of a 'preventative' strategy, Statements can be written for very young children. These two factors alone will cause special educational needs expenditure to rise even if the number of new Statements issued does not increase. This is an expenditure 'time bomb' for some LEAs which is not always acknowledged sufficiently and which makes the control of the special educational needs budget so difficult to achieve (Coopers and Lybrand, 1996).

Currently, most LEAs are attempting to reduce the number of Statements they issue but, on the whole, are meeting opposition from schools. Whatever the level of Statementing within an authority and whatever the exact procedures used for assessments for Statements, more Statements mean more resources for schools. While schools may not want to take on additional children with Statements, most would like more Statements for the children currently on roll. Inevitably LEAs are seeking ways both to change schools' attitudes towards Statements and to change the actual procedures involved. There is a finite amount of money available in any local authority's education budget, and the issuing of an over-large number of Statements eats into that budget considerably. The consequence of this is expressed very clearly in the plans for modification of LMS procedures in a non-metropolitan authority where a much larger-than-average number of Statements had been written since the introduction of the process in 1983, and where this already high figure had increased further since 1990. The document pointed out that, in a cash-limited budget, the additional cost has been met at the expense of school budgets. A Statement does provide a formalized way of defining an individual pupil's needs and how they are to be met, but it is an inflexible and bureaucratic means of achieving this objective. The growth in the number of Statements has led to an unacceptable 'resource gap' between the pupils who do have a Statement and those who just fail to meet the criteria. The comparison is a stark one – the average cost of a mainstream Statement is £3,200 whilst the special educational needs Supplement within the LMS formula provides only £47 for each pupil at Stage 3 of the Code of Practice! These figures make it very clear why schools want Statements and the extent to which Statements directly take money away from other types of provision.

It is not surprising that this LEA sought a solution to the problem of the high level of Statementing. After a process of consultation with schools it was agreed that a strategy for reducing the reliance on State-ments of special educational needs should be implemented. In particular, this involved the devolution of additional funds to schools for non-Statemented special educational needs, according to the number of pupils assessed as being at Stage 3 and above of the Code of Practice and, more unusually, that schools be asked to make a con-tribution of £500 per annum for each new Statement issued. There was, however, the 'safety net' of full LEA funding for what were termed 'high value Statements'. In this way it was ensured that schools would not be deterred from seeking Statements for children with high levels of need (arguably the only pupils who should need Statements at all) but it also emphasized the need to reconsider whether a Statement was appropriate for other children. In the first eighteen months of the introduction of this scheme the level of

Statementing had not actually fallen, but the rise had been stemmed and there was optimism over the longer-term prospects.

Traditionally this authority had not defined an appropriate level of Statementing and it was felt that this was a very significant cause of the ever-increasing number of Statements. There was agreement during the consultation process that the LEA should define a proportion of the school population as being likely to have a level of special need which requires a Statement, but the LEA suggestion of 2% was considered to be too low and no agreement was reached on a precise figure. Nevertheless the most important consensus, that on the need for a reduction in Statements, was reached. This is just one example of an innovative strategy to achieve this aim; most LEAs have the same objective though their methods of attempting to achieve it are very varied.

It is significant that this arrangement was arrived at after a process of major consultation with schools. The original proposal for what schools regarded as 'paying for Statements' was not popular but, in only slightly modified form, was eventually agreed upon. It indicates the success of an approach recommended by Coopers and Lybrand which pointed out the advantages of consultation and transparency in dealings between schools and the LEAs. It was lack of transparency in dealings with the authority, especially in relation to Statements, of which the heads in our study were most critical.

NON-STATEMENTED SPECIAL EDUCATIONAL NEEDS

Although it is Statements and Statemented children that are often the centre of attention they are, of course, a small proportion of the total number of children who are regarded as having special educational needs. Despite the changes in the law, the terminology, the relationships between schools and LEAs, the increased control of budgets by schools and so on, many aspects of the definition of, and the provision for, special educational needs remained basically similar over time. The first identification of pupils with special educational needs is usually in the classroom, and the subsequent provision to meet these needs is the concern of the school with the LEA, in the form of support services, becoming involved when the school is finding it difficult to cope alone. There have, however, been significant changes in how these arrangements are managed. When the first *One in Five* study was conducted, policy and procedures were, on the whole, much less formal, though there were variations both between individual schools and between LEAs. At the end of the 1990s, mainly as a result of changes in law, all aspects of special educational needs provision have become more formalized and this process continues. There are however, as has been emphasized before, still considerable variations between LEAs. There are many ways of organizing the allocation of resources for special educational needs provision in mainstream schools, but for most LEAs there will be two key issues: how much funding to delegate or devolve to schools above the minimum requirements, and how to arrive at a satisfactory formula for calculating special educational needs supplements for schools to receive as part of their delegated budget.

The exact arrangements under which LMS schemes operate are detailed and complex and not our present concern, but schools are expected to provide for most special educational needs from their delegated budgets, control of which is in the hands of the school, while at the same time the LEA is itself responsible for ensuring that the special educational needs of pupils in its schools are met. Finding the right balance between retaining control of funds centrally to provide help through support services for schools and pupils which is free to schools, devolving funds to schools which have to be spent on special educational needs (often through extra help provided by the LEA support services) and delegating budgets to schools which are used at the schools' discretion, is fraught with difficulties. There would appear to be a tendency among LEAs to favour delegating funds to schools, but including a special needs supplement within this budget in recognition of the fact that special educational needs are spread unequally among schools. Details of the procedures used by one non-metropolitan authority to calculate the special educational needs supplement illustrates the factors involved.

The special educational needs of pupils will normally be met from within the Base Allocation and Pupil Allocation. However, in order to recognise the variation in the level of special educational needs from school to school supplements will be allocated as follows:

The *first element* will allocate an amount for each pupil on roll at the January Form 7 count.

The *second element* will consist of two indices:

i) the number of pupils who were entitled to free school meals, averaged over three years;

ii) the number of pupils assessed as being at Stage 2 and at Stages 3, 4 or 5 of the CoP.

The calculation of the second element will be very straight-forward:

a) number of free school meal entitlements, averaged over 3 years multiplied by £x.
b) number of pupils at Stage 2 of the CoP multiplied by £y.
c) number of pupils at Stage 3, 4 or 5 of the CoP multiplied by £z.

From this document it can be seen that the largest part of the allocation is based simply on pupil numbers, but there is an additional element that is based in part on free school meal entitlement and partly on the actual numbers of pupils identified as having special educational needs. There is continued debate over whether it is best to use 'proxy' indicators, of which free school meals is the most popular, or measures of actual levels of special educational needs. On the one hand free school meals, although strongly correlated with special educational needs, is not identical to it. Consequently it lacks accuracy, but on the other hand, it is correlated and is a very easy measure to use. If an LEA wants to use 'real' special educational needs numbers then, it is necessary to define clearly the characteristics of pupils with every type of special educational needs at each Stage of the Code of Practice and ensure that these numbers are adhered to. Many LEAs have introduced such systems through conducting a full audit of special educational needs with their schools and introducing a system of motivation to ensure that the system is applied equally through the authority. This is a difficult and costly business and still does not solve the problem of the level and type of resources required to meet each sort of need. In particular it can produce problems of 'negative incentives': that is, if resources follow need, then the more pupils with special educational needs a school has, the more resources it gets; but if it succeeds in reducing this number, then it will lose resources. This is clearly an unsatisfactory state of affairs and can only be combated through more elaborate procedures. In the case indicated the authority has adopted the strategy of using both direct and proxy indications of need, which is probably the best in the circumstances.

LEAs are struggling to make resource allocation for special educational needs work as best they can within the framework of the current arrangements, but it is an extremely bureaucratic and complex system. It is hard not to sympathize with the LEA officer who asked us, 'How on earth did we get into this mess?' Like all managers and administrators he knows that he has to start from where he is and that this is usually not where he would like to be starting from. These are difficult issues for LEAs, and they are not just issues of administrative procedures but also involve fundamental questions about the nature and extent of special needs and the purposes being served by special provision. The empirical data we are considering on special needs in schools and an analysis of the relationship between policy, administrative procedures and practice in schools is clearly relevant to any attempt to address these questions.

—9

Conclusion

The main aim of the research study which forms the basis of this book was to provide a representative account of special educational needs in mainstream primary schools at the end of the 1990s. An analysis of various features of the picture of special needs to emerge, together with a comparison with a similar study, conducted in the same schools in the early 1980s, has been related to various themes to emerge from education policy developments and from theoretical considerations of the concept of special educational needs. In this final chapter we shall first give a brief overview of some of the central empirical findings from the work. We shall then consider some theoretical perspectives on these findings and their relationship to ongoing debates in educational thinking and education policy. Finally we shall put forward some suggestions about the practical implications of the research, both for practice at classroom and school level and for the development of education policy nationally and locally.

The core empirical finding from the research relates to the prevalence of special educational needs overall and of different kinds, and the comparison between the 1998 figures and those from 1981. In summary, just over a quarter of all children in mainstream Key Stage 2 classrooms were on the Register of special educational needs in 1998, a very considerable increase compared with the already substantial figure from 1981. The great majority of these children, almost 90%, had difficulties with learning, and difficulties of this kind showed the greatest degree of increase since the earlier study. Emotional and behavioural difficulties, including discipline problems, had also increased, but not to the same extent as learning difficulties. Health, sensory and physical difficulties had remained at the same level as in 1981. As before, there was a considerable degree of overlap between these categories, and many children had more than one type of special educational need.

We started the research with the question which provides the subtitle of this book: *One in Five?* We wanted to know if the picture of just under 20% of children being regarded as having special needs which emerged from the 1981 survey was still true in the late 1990s. The evidence shows that it is no longer the case and that 'One in four' represents the level of special needs in mainstream primary schools. Unlike the earlier figure, this can be regarded as an 'official' level of special needs, in that these children have been formally classified as having such needs on the special educational needs Register. The increase in prevalence is principally about learning. Despite a good deal of attention paid recently to claims about increasing levels of emotional and behavioural difficulties in schools and increasing levels of disruptive behaviour, the increase in emotional and behavioural difficulties and discipline problems is very much less than the increase in learning difficulties.

The headteachers of the schools in the study attributed the increase which they had observed in the prevalence of special educational needs in their schools to two factors. For some heads it represented an increase in social difficulties and levels of poverty creating increased difficulties in schools. An even larger number however attributed it to changes in school and LEA procedures which resulted in more children being identified. Other evidence from the present study lends some support to this latter argument. There is no evidence of a systematic change over time in the levels of difficulty of children being identified as having problems with learning; but there is some evidence of children whose difficulties are less extreme being more consistently identified than previously. The evidence from the present study strongly confirms the association between social deprivation and special educational needs. Of course this is not the same as demonstrating that social changes are responsible for the changes over time.

Schools and classrooms showed considerable variation in the proportion of pupils having special educational needs. At the extremes there were schools with less than 10% of their pupils and schools with over half their pupils on the Register. Nevertheless, as in the earlier study, most schools are concentrated towards the middle of the distribution and there is no tendency for schools to become polarized into schools with and schools without special educational needs. It was clear that such needs were very widespread through the educational system and are issues for all schools and all teachers. This was widely recognized by the teachers and headteachers in the study.

Boys outnumbered girls among children with special educational needs by almost two to one. Despite the recent attention to the under-achievement of boys and the suggestions that this is a growing problem, the ratio of boys to girls had decreased very slightly compared with 1981. Boys are not increasingly identified as having special educational needs compared with girls, although they are very considerably over-represented. There is some evidence of a slight tendency for boys to be 'over-identified' as having learning difficulties; the reading scores of boys with learning difficulties were slightly higher than those of girls.

Pupils from ethnic minority backgrounds were not over-represented among children with special educational needs (although this result is based on aggregating data on pupils from very diverse backgrounds). This was a change from the 1981 survey where such pupils were over-represented and means that, unlike majority pupils, the proportion of children from minorities with special needs has decreased. A rather different situation applies to children from Afro-Caribbean backgrounds. These pupils were very slightly over-represented compared with white pupils. They were less likely to be described as having learning problems than their white peers but were considerably more likely to be described as having emotional and behavioural difficulties and, to some extent, as posing discipline problems. Afro-Caribbean pupils have been the focus of a good deal of concern both with regard to under-achievement and as victims of racism within the education system. The figures here provide no evidence of particular achievement problems, but they do support concerns about perceptions of the behaviour of some pupils in teachers' and schools' response to them. More encouragingly, the extent of such difficulties has decreased since 1981 and the gap between Afro-Caribbean pupils and others has narrowed very considerably. It is also the case that the great majority of pupils, from whatever background, are not regarded as problems by their teachers.

The variation between schools was strongly related to the overall levels of academic performance in the school, as measured by National Curriculum assessments, and to levels of deprivation in the communities they served, as measured by the proportions of children receiving free school meals. The very strong correlation between the Year 6 assessment results and special educational needs reinforces the continuity between special needs and low achievement more generally, and the complex relationship between special needs and overall standards of achievement. Overall achievement levels were correlated not only with learning difficulties but, just as strongly, with emotional and behavioural problems. The impact of social deprivation on special educational needs was, for the most part, mediated through the relationship between this measure and overall achievement. In most areas deprivation did not impact on special needs except through its influence on achievement generally. The exception to this pattern was in the area of discipline problems. Here there was a strong association between poverty, measured by the level of free school meals, and the level of discipline problems, regardless of levels of achievement.

Schools provide support for children with special needs in a variety of ways. These involve a combination of in-class and out-of-class support and a combination of class teacher, support teacher and learning support/assistant support. A majority of children with special needs get support within the classroom but this is mainly just from the class teacher. About 40% of these children get other in-class support, mainly from a classroom assistant or learning support assistant in a mixture of one-to-one and small group situations. About half of all children with special needs are withdrawn from the class for support. In about half of cases this is work with a specialist support teacher, in about 10% of cases with the special educational needs co-ordinator and in just over a third of cases with a learning support assistant. About three-quarters of all children getting help are getting it for reading and literacy, with a minority getting help with numeracy. Support in other areas of the curriculum or for behaviour is much less common.

A slightly smaller proportion of pupils with special needs were withdrawn from the classroom for support in 1998 compared with 1981. However, because of the expansion of special needs this represented a higher proportion of all children in the class. In all, nearly one in eight of the children in mainstream classes spend some time withdrawn from the class. For 60% of children this represented two hours or less in the school week, and only for 4% of children did it amount to more than the equivalent of an hour a day.

The role of special educational needs co-ordinator was created by the 1993 Education Act. This is essentially a new role and no direct equivalent existed at the time of the first study, though it was not unusual for a school to have a teacher with special responsibility for special educational needs. The creation of this role is one aspect of the formalization of many aspects of special educational needs provision that has taken place over the last twenty years. The Code of Practice has created what some co-ordinators regard as 'a mountain of paperwork', particularly the keeping of records of all pupils on the Register and Individual Education Plans for pupils on Stage 2 and above. Perhaps rather surprisingly there was considerable support and a fair amount of enthusiasm among class teachers for their school's system of record-keeping. Ninety per cent of teachers were happy with the system they used and 30% of them regarded it as *very* useful. There were frequent comments from teachers praising the work of their co-ordinator and saying how useful they found the detailed records of children compiled by the co-ordinator. Individual Education Plans met with a more mixed response. Although almost all the co-ordinators thought they were of some use, nearly half expressed serious reservations, mostly about the time involved; but there were educational objections as well.

Policy and practice in implementing the Code of Practice varied considerably between schools and particularly between LEAs, but whatever the detailed nature of the procedure, moving children between Stages was a serious undertaking with considerable resource implications. Most systems of resource allocation include substantial additional funding for children on Stage 3, when support services are usually involved. The schools had mixed reactions to the help they received from these services, including the school psychological service, but there was a widespread desire to receive more help, especially from the learning and behaviour support services and the school psychological service. Children with the most severe needs are Statemented and this is usually accompanied by a very substantial increase in resources. LEAs are concerned about the level of Statementing and most would like it to be reduced, but schools would often like more of their pupils to have a Statement. Over 60% of the headteachers in the survey said that they would like to have more Statements for pupils currently in their schools.

The issue of Statementing was one of a number of areas over which headteachers were critical of the policy and practice of their LEAs. Of most concern was the level of resourcing: 80% of heads felt that they had inadequate resources to meet the special needs of all their pupils, but they also felt that many of the LEAs' procedures were unnecessarily bureaucratic and time-consuming and also lacked the transparency needed to build better relations.

The LEAs are not unaware of these issues but they face major problems in relation to special needs provision. There is a finite pot of money that can be spent on special needs provision and several education officers expressed serious concerns over their authority's ability to stop the special education budget from spiralling out of control. While it is proving very difficult to reduce the number of special schools in the face of parental opposition to closure, the demands from mainstream schools grow as they put more children on the Register and press for Statements for more children. This situation is particularly difficult to manage during a period of local government reorganization in which the new Unitary Authorities were created; however, many of the problems faced may be exaggerated by organizational change but are not created by it. Local authorities have a particular responsibility for provision for special needs and it is at LEA level that the problems created by the definition of special educational needs in terms of provision are most keenly felt.

The issue of inclusion of all children in mainstream schools does not have a prominent position in thinking in primary schools. Headteachers and teachers did not have a commitment to inclusion as an educational principle and virtually unanimously saw a continuing role for special schools, especially in the case of children with emotional and behavioural difficulties. Nevertheless, in the case of most children currently in their schools there was a firm commitment from teachers that this was the right placement. This extended to the majority of children with Statements of special educational needs and others with severe difficulties. Many of these children would be in special schools in some circumstances. There is therefore a good deal of inclusive practice in the schools in the study.

One of the major findings of the *One in Five* study was that the concept of special educational need found immediate resonance with teachers. Primary schoolteachers knew what was meant by the term, and when they applied it to the children in their classes they agreed with the Warnock Committee's estimation that about 18% of pupils in their classes had special educational needs. Although these estimates were arrived at in different ways – one being based on epidemiological studies and expert opinion and the other on professional personal classroom experience – the very fact of agreement seemed highly significant as it indicated that future use of the term as a basis for policy and provision would chime with teachers' notions of the situation and there was a good chance that policy and practice could progress in harmony. There appeared to be strong indications of a consensus on these important issues.

There seemed to be a general eagerness to abandon the term 'handicapped' and its perceived pejorative overtones and a willingness to substitute 'special educational needs' and subsequently apply it to a very much larger group of children. There are however problems with the idea of a continuum of special need, for although it is possible to see the '2%' and the '20%' as being on a continuum, there is a line drawn between the '20%' and the rest. If such a line is drawn at the 20% mark it will be the case that most of that 20% have more in common with the 80% (who are not an homogenous group) than they do with the 2% who are not an homogenous group either. The usefulness of the term 'special educational needs' can be questioned both analytically and practically. On the one hand, by considering the 20% together as one group the very serious difficulties experienced by the 2% can appear to be diminished while the differences between the 18% and the 80% can be exaggerated. In terms of provision this can lead to an underestimation of just how special the needs of a small number of pupils are but, at the same time, can it be sensible to regard 18% of pupils as having special needs? It could be argued that if this large number of pupils do indeed have special needs they must be so regarded, but at this point the problematic nature of the whole concept has to be considered. There are pupils who experience a whole range of learning and other difficulties, but special educational needs is also a social construct and, at least up to a point, pupils have special needs because we say they have special needs. There is no objective definition of what constitutes special educational needs and the term can be applied very flexibly. The schools in the 1998 study regarded 26% of their pupils as having special educational needs and this increase to over a quarter of all children calls into question still further the appropriateness and the usefulness of regarding such a high number of children as needing 'special' provision.

The whole notion of 'extra' provision is highly problematic. What exactly counts as 'extra' provision and what exactly is this provision extra to? On the one hand it is clear that a child who has the full-time help of a classroom assistant and is also withdrawn from the classroom for several hours a week for literacy work in a small group with a specialist support teacher is receiving 'extra' help; that is, assistance that is additional to that which is enjoyed by most pupils in that school. On the other hand, the position of the child whom the class teacher 'keeps an eye on' is much more ambiguous.

These problems were always inherent in the definitions of special educational need and remain unresolved. In the Warnock Report need was defined in terms of provision that is additional or extra to what is generally available without any consideration of either more independent definitions of need or any notion of 'general availability'. This opens the way for a limitless number of children to demand an infinite amount of extra provision. In retrospect this appears to be a recipe for disaster. Subsequent legislation has not basically changed this position and the whole issue of resourcing special educational needs provision is still fraught with problems and it is difficult to see any real resolution under the present system.

The connection between the definition of special educational needs and the requirement for 'extra' provision is shown to be particularly problematic when the very large numbers of pupils regarded as having special educational needs are considered. A quarter of 7- to 11-year-olds may have educational needs that require provision, if we want to use this sort of terminology, but how can such a large proportion of pupils be regarded as needing anything 'special', unless we regard the education of all children in that way? If the performance of such a large number of children is regarded as problematic then this must be regarded as a general educational issue, not an issue of identifying individuals with particular special needs. There have been many expressions of concern over educational standards in the UK (Alexander *et al.*, 1992) and international comparative studies identify the low achievement of a substantial proportion of pupils in our schools as problematic (Prais, 1993). Low achievement and special educational needs, though clearly connected, tend to be viewed very differently. The low achievement of a large number of school students is seen as a failure of the education system whereas special educational needs can, at least in some measure, be seen as a failure of children, something with which schools have to cope and which has its origins outside the school. This perspective on special educational needs was made very clear by teachers when discussing the aetiology of the special educational needs of individual pupils.

Underlying the provision for pupils with special educational needs there are two main trends that lead in contradictory directions and are not easily reconciled. One emphasizes the uniqueness of individuals and their need for differentiated provision, while the other concentrates on the similarities between learners and, at primary school, the similarity of educational goals, while recognizing that there are going to be a small number of exceptions.

The first approach stresses that all learners are unique and should be so treated; in effect advocating a version of individual education plans for all. Underpinning this idea is that, at the same time as we are unique beings, we are also all the same in that we are all different and require different things. If everyone is treated differently, then the distinction between those who receive the same or very similar provision to each other and those who receive very different provision is diminished. As there is no emphasis on the grouping together of individuals who may be experiencing similar problems and everyone is treated as an individual, there is no reason why all needs cannot be met in the same location.

This idea of the uniqueness of individuals is not, of course, new but has been present for some time in work in the special educational needs context and more generally. Hegarty and Pocklington (1981) and Hodgson *et al.* (1984) argued that the approach more frequently found in special educational needs provision of the highly individualized variety could profitably be used much more widely. This basic position is elaborated by Ainscow (1993). They all start with the issue of what is required to satisfy special educational needs and then move on to conclude that it is the type of provision that should be more generally available in schools.

The desirability of individualized learning for all is also argued for in a totally different context. Bentley (1998) has argued that a combination of advances in learning theory and the increasing sophistication and availability of information technology will soon result in a totally different approach to all aspects of learning, education and schooling. Although there is no special reference made here to people with learning and other difficulties, the extreme individuality of the approach to learning does automatically apply to all. Although coming from very different starting points and, for the most part, concentrating on different issues, they end up at much the same place with a high level of individualization of provision accompanied by considerable personal choice.

In very marked contrast there are numerous studies on the connection between teaching style, approaches to classroom learning and pupil performance that suggest that, at least for most pupils, increased individualization is not the way ahead. Findings from the ORACLE studies, for example, point to the benefits of whole-class teaching in the primary school (Galton *et al.*, 1980). This was again brought to prominence more recently in the studies of international comparisons of educational standards which indicated that high standards at primary school level are strongly associated with whole-class teaching; all pupils in the class learning the same things at the same time (Reynolds and Farrell, 1996). In these studies no particular attention was directed at those students with the most severe difficulties; instead overall standards in mainstream schools were the focus of attention. However, as the proportion of pupils with special needs is so high, and the vast majority of these children have learning difficulties, issues relevant to overall educational standards must also be relevant to these pupils.

As with the first group of studies discussed, the implications for practice of this second group of studies are also less distinction between special educational needs and other provision, but here the similarity ends. Instead of all students having individualized work plans, all students, or nearly all students, at least in the primary school, would do the same work, the argument being that despite their all being unique individuals, they all share the same educational needs. All pupils, for instance, need to learn to read and any improvement in methods of teaching reading will benefit all, or nearly all, children and possibly prevent difficulties from arising. In many ways this is a compelling argument and is well backed up by research, the problem with this approach centring around the proviso already made about its application to 'nearly all' rather than absolutely all children. If overall standards are to be raised by treating children in the same way then, it is difficult to escape the conclusion that a small number of children have needs too different to be accommodated within this common framework. This would not, of course, mean that they could not be educated in mainstream schools, but it would mean that they would not share all the same classroom experiences.

These are all issues that seriously affect not only the type of provision that schools make for pupils currently regarded as having special educational needs, but also for all other pupils. On the one hand they can go for ever-increasing differentiation, heading in the direction of a truly individualized learning experience that accommodates all students. On the other hand schools could opt for a 'whole-class' approach, emphasizing a shared experience and shared goals, while making special provision for the small number of pupils who cannot benefit from this approach. In practice, strict adherence to either of these approaches would be regarded as extreme and in virtually all schools different elements of policy and provision will reflect these different approaches. However, the two approaches are so different that attempts to use bits of one and bits of the other are bound to result in unresolved tensions. Current government policy displays these tensions; for instance, the Literacy and Numeracy Hours emphasize commonality of experience while the requirement to write Individual Education Plans for large numbers of pupils emphasizes individualization and differentiation.

Gerber sees basically the same conflicts present within the wider education system (Gerber, 1996). He argues that special education and mass public education conflict in a fundamental way. Mass public education is based on the notion of providing equality of opportunity; that is, providing access so that advantage can be taken *of what is provided*. To achieve its ambitious aim of universality, Gerber argues, public schooling largely ignores individual differences that contribute to variable instructional outcomes. On the other hand, special education has been concerned *mostly* with individuals and how they might be accommodated by institutional transformations. 'In many ways, special education's explicit concern for individual differences has been the source of its moral strength, but also its fatal political weakness' (p. 157). When the two systems are brought together, conflicts are likely to arise, particularly over differential funding and organizational upheaval. These areas of conflict were apparent in the study schools and LEAs, especially in relation to resourcing. Many schools felt that both the overall level of funding for special educational needs provision that they received was inadequate and also that the procedures required were inefficient and burdensome. From the LEA's point of view an ever-increasing amount of professional time and energy is spent in contriving ways in which to prevent the special educational needs budget from spiralling out of control.

In Chapter 1 we emphasized the importance of numbers: of the prevalence and distribution of special educational needs of various kinds in determining education policy and provision. We also emphasized that these numbers were not simply given but were created from the interaction between the difficulties children experience in schools and the perceptions and responses of their schools and teachers. In this sense the actions of teachers create educational policy and the circumstances in which it is made, as well as acting as implementers of policy. The sort of large-scale empirical study reported here provides an opportunity to view special educational needs issues from the perspective of a large and representative sample of teachers and to consider the implications of these perspectives for policy development.

One lesson to emerge from the study is the importance of addressing explicitly the tensions between the commonalities in educational provision and the uniqueness and individuality of the educational services that some children need. We have already suggested that we should reconsider the educational value of regarding a quarter of pupils in mainstream schools as having special educational needs. Such needs are logically indistinguishable from the educational difficulties of all lower-achieving children in schools. Many of these children have their needs met by the class teacher as part of his or her ordinary work in the classroom; other children are described by their class teachers as neither receiving anything special nor needing anything special, despite being on the Register of special educational needs.

All this suggests that the bureaucratic and time-consuming procedures of the Code of Practice may be inappropriate for a substantial proportion of the children to whom they apply. We need to be sure that children's educational experiences are being improved in order to justify the resources such procedures absorb but, for many children at Stage 1 of the Register, it is not being affected at all.

The current procedures with their highly individualized emphasis may also distract attention from the importance of the routine of classroom instruction and management for meeting children's needs. At school level it would be appropriate to regard special needs policies as less distinct than they sometimes are at present and to subsume much of them under achievement policies. The very individualized concept of special educational needs also tends to obscure the strong association between such needs and levels of poverty in the communities served by schools.

The study has shown the enduring popularity of withdrawal from the regular class as a strategy for meeting special educational needs, especially those connected with learning. This is a strategy which many teachers value and is virtually universal in the schools in the study. This is a case in which teachers and schools have effectively made policy on special needs provision. It was also the area of provision where it was most clear what it was that children with special needs were receiving.

Headteachers and special educational needs co-ordinators are very aware of the extent to which the Stages of the Code of Practice drive resources at both school and LEA level. Much of the pressure to assess children for Stage 3 of the Register and to provide Statements of special educational needs, comes not from a requirement for more information about what a child needs, but as a way of accessing additional resources for the child. This is a problem which emerged almost immediately Statements were introduced in 1983. The Code of Practice has extended the problem so that it now applies to a much greater number of pupils. The pressure for more Statements and to move children to Stage 3 is almost entirely resource driven. Schools and LEAs need to think about ways of distinguishing between the educational information they need about a child and the resource allocation procedures they operate.

Learning difficulties are by far the most common type of special educational need. Nevertheless, more than one in ten of the children on the special educational needs Register do not have learning difficulties. For many more, learning difficulties are combined with other types of problems and may not be the major element of the child's needs or the reason for the child being on the Register. Although problems of health and behaviour may sometimes be the main reason for difficulties in learning, teachers only thought this to be the case for a small proportion of children. It may be useful to consider whether the term 'special educational needs' is appropriate for children whose main difficulties are not difficulties in learning. If these children were not on the special needs Register this would help to reinforce the connection between special educational needs and low achievement and between special needs policies and achievement policies.

As we have seen, the development of an appropriate framework for meeting children's educational needs is a complex and demanding enterprise. The teachers and headteachers we talked to were highly committed and highly professional in their attempts to meet the needs of the children for whom they were responsible. Within the Code of Practice and other aspects of current procedures for managing special needs provision, it is almost inevitable that the concerns of teachers will lead to even greater pressure for more Statements, for children to be moved to higher Stages of the Register and for more children to be regarded as having special educational needs. The overview of provision and prevalence which this study has provided suggests that this is not the best way forward. Policies which pay attention to the common needs of children and ways of meeting them in schools, and which lead to fewer children needing to be formally identified as having special educational needs, would help to give a clearer focus to special needs provision.

Appendix

The data on special educational needs in primary schools presented here are based on structured personal interviews with a sample of headteachers, class teachers and special educational needs co-ordinators in schools serving Key Stage 2 pupils (children aged 7 to 11). The design of the 1998 survey was largely determined by the need to replicate the 1981 study.

In 1981 a stratified random sample was drawn of 61 primary schools. The schools were located in ten local education authorities, six of which were county authorities, three metropolitan authorities and one London Borough. These proportions reflected the numbers of pupils educated in authorities of each type. In seven authorities five schools were sampled at random within a stratification system reflecting school size. In two authorities ten schools were sampled in the same way, and in one authority six schools were sampled. Only schools with what were then called 'junior' classes were included. Ten, rather than five, schools were sampled in two of the authorities as these were to be the focus of an additional observational stage of the research, not repeated in 1998. An additional school was included in one LEA to represent a particular type of provision. In these 61 schools interviews were requested with all headteachers, class teachers of 7 to 11 year olds and what were then called remedial teachers.

In 1998 50 of the 61 schools were approached and asked to participate in a similar survey. This design required five schools from each of the ten original LEAs, eliminating the over-representation in some LEAs by omitting schools at random. Forty-four of the original 50 schools agreed to take part. If two schools in an LEA were not able to take part they were replaced by as similar schools as possible. If only one school in an LEA dropped out it was not replaced. In one LEA a school in the original sample initially refused to participate and later agreed to be included, but only after two other schools had been approached. The final sample of 48 schools therefore includes two which would not have been included if the research design had been followed exactly. Detailed data on pupils were not collected in these two schools. Therefore, while the information from the teacher and headteacher interviews is based on a sample of 48 schools, the data on pupils is based on a sample of 46.

An important feature of both the 1981 and the 1998 surveys was the exceptionally high response rate both from institutions and from individuals. In 1981 the response rate from schools was 96.7% and all headteachers in the final sample agreed to be interviewed. The 428 class teachers interviewed were 97.3% of the teachers of junior-age classes in the schools. (The rather informal arrangements often existing for remedial teaching at the time makes it impossible to give response rates for these teachers. The 37 remedial teachers interviewed must be regarded as an opportunity sample.) In 1998 the response rate from the original sample of schools was 88%. In the schools in the final sample all headteachers and 46 of the special educational needs co-ordinators (95.8%) were interviewed. The 299 classteachers interviewed were from 95.5% of the Key Stage 2 classes in the schools. As far as could be judged, all non-response was connected with illness, other absences and problems with making arrangements rather than unwillingness to take part in the study. These response rates are particularly important in a study concerned to give a representative picture of the situation in schools and classrooms. The sample is on a large enough scale to be generalized and we can be confident that there could only be a very small biasing effect from a systematic difference between participants and non-participants.

All data was collected through structured personal interviews, usually lasting between 40 minutes and one hour. This appoach to data gathering means that exactly comparable information can be obtained from all those interviewed, but the presence of the interviewer means that individual personal responses could also be included. An important aspect of the class-teacher interviews, following the procedure used in 1981, was that information was obtained on the needs of and provision for specific children. Teachers were not asked to generalize about the special needs of children or the best ways of meeting them. They were asked about the needs of children in their classes at the time and the ways they were being met.

As is very common in educational research, the sample design was nested rather than being a simple random sample of teachers. That is, LEAs were sampled first, then schools within them and within schools all teachers were interviewed. As well as being a more efficient use of resources than a simple random sample, this sort of design also has strengths with regard to the type of analyses that are possible. The perspectives of individual teachers can be located in the context of the school in which they work rather than being entirely individual. Similarly, school policies and procedures can be located in the context of LEA policies and the availability of various sorts of services and resources locally. In both 1981 and 1998 interviews were conducted with LEA officers in order to provide an LEA context for the data obtained from headteachers and teachers. In 1998 it was not possible to replicate this aspect of the earlier study exactly as the reorganization of local government meant that some LEAs no longer existed in their previous form. In particular, all but one of the original six county authorities had been affected by reorganization to some degree. In most cases it was possible to identify an obvious successor authority in which most of the sample schools were located. The 48 schools in the 1998 sample were from fifteen LEAs and in some of the reorganized LEAs there was only one school in an authority. The study does not address the issue of any influence of this reorganization on special educational provision.

References

Ainscow, M. (1993) *Towards Effective Schools for All: A Reconsideration of the Special Needs Task*. Tamworth: NASEN.

Alexander, R., Rose, J. and Woodhead, C. (1992) *Curriculum Organisation and Classroom Practice in Primary Schools*. London: DES.

Archer, M. (1979) *The Social Origins of Educational Systems*. London: Sage.

Archer, M. (1981) 'Educational Politics: a Model for their Analysis.' In Broadfoot, P., Brock, C. and Tulasiewicz, W. (eds) *Politics and Educational Change*. London: Croom Helm.

Armstrong, D. (1995) *Power and Partnership in Education*. London: Routledge.

Bangs, J. (1993) 'Support Services: Stability or Erosion?' *British Journal of Special Education* 20.3, 105–7.

Barton, L. (ed.) (1988) *The Politics of Special Educational Needs*. Lewes: Falmer Press.

Bennett, N. (1976) *Teaching Styles and Pupil Progress*. London: Open Books.

Bentley, T. (1998) *Learning Beyond the Classroom*. London: Routledge.

Clark, C., Dyson, A. and Millward, A. (1998) 'Theorising Special Education: Time to Move On?' In Clark, C., Dyson, A. and Millward, A. (eds) *Theorising Special Education*. London: Routledge.

Coopers and Lybrand (1996) *The Special Educational Needs Initiative*. London: Coopers and Lybrand.

Craske, M.-L. (1988) 'Learned Helplessness, Self-worth Motivation and Attribution Retraining for Primary School Children.' *British Journal of Educational Psychology* 58, 152–64.

Croll, P. (1996a) 'Practitioners or Policy Makers? Models of Teachers and Educational Change'. In Croll, P. (ed.) *Teachers, Pupils and Primary Schooling*. London: Cassell.

Croll, P. (1996b) 'A Curriculum for All? Special Educational Needs and the National Curriculum'. In Croll, P. (ed.) *Teachers, Pupils and Primary Schooling*. London: Cassell.

Croll, P. and Moses, D. (1985) *One in Five*. London: Routledge and Kegan Paul.

Croll, P. and Moses, D. (1989) 'Policy and Practice in Education: The Implementation of the 1981 Education Act in England and Wales'. In Brown, R. and Chazan, M. (eds) *Learning Difficulties and Emotional Problems*. Calgary: Detselig.

Croll, P. and Moses, D. (1998) 'Pragmatism, Ideology and Educational Change: The Case of Special Educational Needs.' *British Journal of Educational Studies* 46.1, 11–25.

Croll, P. and Moses, D. (1999) 'Continuity and Change in Special Education

Provision: Some Perspectives on Local Education Authority Decision Making.' *British Educational Research Journal* 25.5.

Croll, P. and Moses, D. (forthcoming) 'Ideologies and Utopias: Special Education Professionals' Views on Inclusion.' *European Journal of Special Needs Education* 15.1.

Davies, J., Garner, P. and Lee, J. (eds) (1998) *Managing Special Needs in Mainstream Schools.* London: David Fulton.

Department for Education (1994) *The Code of Practice on the Identification and Assessment of Special Educational Needs.* London: DFE.

Department for Education and Employment (1997) *Excellence for All Children: Meeting Special Educational Needs.* A Green Paper. London: DfEE.

Department for Education and Employment (1998) *Meeting Special Educational Needs: A Programme of Action.* London: DfEE.

Department for Education and Employment (1999) *Meeting the Challenge: Education Action Zones.* London: DfEE.

Department of Education and Science (1967) *Children and their Primary Schools* (The Plowden Report). London: HMSO.

Department of Education and Science (1978) *The Education of Handicapped Children and Young People* (The Warnock Report). London: HMSO.

Department of Education and Science (1981a) *Education Act 1981.* London: HMSO.

Department of Education and Science (1981b) *Circular No 8/81.* London: HMSO.

Douglas, J. W. B. (1967) *The Home and the School.* St Albans: Panther.

Evans, W. (1998) 'The Problems of Interpretation and Guidance: the Consequences of SENCO Action from a Legal Point of View.' In Davies, J., Garner, P. and Lee, J. (eds) *Managing Special Needs in Mainstream Schools.* London: David Fulton.

Evans, J. and Lunt, I. (1993) 'Special Educational Provision after LMS.' *British Journal of Special Education* 20.2, 59–62.

Fletcher-Campbell, F. (1993) *LEA Support for Special Needs.* Windsor: NFER-Nelson.

Fletcher-Campbell, F. (1994) *Still Joining Forces?* Windsor: NFER.

Fletcher-Campbell, F. (1996) *The Resourcing of Special Educational Needs.* Windsor: NFER.

Floud, J. and Halsey, A. H. (1957) 'Intelligence Tests, Social Class and Selection for Secondary Schools.' *British Journal of Sociology* 8.1.

Fulcher, G. (1989) *Disabling Policies? A Comparative Approach to Education Policy and Disability.* Lewes: Falmer Press.

Galton, M. and Simon, B. (eds) (1980) *Progress and Performance in the Primary Classroom.* London: Routledge and Kegan Paul.

Galton, M., Simon, B. and Croll, P. (1980) *Inside the Primary Classroom.* London: Routledge and Kegan Paul.

Gerber, M. (1996) 'Reforming Special Education: Beyond Inclusion.' In Christenson, C. and Rizvi, F. *Disability and the Dilemmas of Education and Justice.* Buckingham: Open University Press.

Gerwirtz, S., Ball, S. and Bowe, R. (1995) *Markets, Choice and Equity in Education.* Buckingham: Open University Press.

Gibson, A. and Asthana, S. (1998) 'Schools, Pupils and Examination Results.' *British Educational Research Journal* 24.3, 269–82

Gillborn, D. and Gipps, C. (1996) *Recent Research on the Achievements of Ethnic Minority Pupils.* London: HMSO.

Goacher, B., Evans, J. Welton, J. and Wedell, K. (1988) *Policy and Provision for Special Educational Needs.* London: Cassell.

162   *References*

Halsey, A. H. and Gardiner, L. (1953) 'Selection for Secondary Education and Achievement in Four Grammar Schools.' *British Journal of Sociology* 4.

Harries, N. (1997) *Special Educational Needs and Access to Justice*. Bristol: Jordans.

Hegarty, S. and Pocklington, K. (1981) *Educating Pupils with Special Needs in the Ordinary School*. Windsor: NFER-Nelson

Hegarty, S. and Moses, D. (eds) (1988) *Developing Expertise*. Windsor: NFER-Nelson.

Hodgson, A., Clunies-Ross, L. and Hegarty, S. (1984) *Learning Together: Teaching Children with Special Educational Needs in the Ordinary School*. Windsor: NFER-Nelson.

Jowett, S., Hegarty, S. and Moses, D. (1988) *Joining Forces: a Study of Links Between Ordinary and Special Schools*. Windsor: NFER-Nelson.

Millward, A. and Skidmore, D. (1995) *Local Authorities' Management of Special Needs*. Report to the Joseph Rowntree Foundation.

Minow, M. (1985) 'Learning to Live with the Dilemmas of Difference.' In Bartlett, K. T. and Wegner, J. W. (eds) *Children with Special Needs*. Boulder: Transaction Books.

Mittler, P. (1993) *Teacher Education for Special Needs*. Tamworth: NASEN.

Mittler, P. and Mittler, H. (1982) *Partnership with Parents*. Stratford on Avon: National Council for Special Education.

Mortimore, P, Sammons, P., Stoll, L., Lewis, D. and Ecob, R. (1988) *School Matters*. London: Open Books.

Moses, D. and Croll, P. (1987) 'Parents as Partners or Problems?' *Disability, Handicap and Society* 2.1, 75–84.

Moses, D., Hegarty, S. and Jowett, S. (1988) *Supporting Ordinary Schools*. Windsor: NFER-Nelson.

National Curriculum Council (1989) *A Curriculum for All*. York: NCC.

Norwich, B. (1993) 'Ideological Dilemmas in Special Needs Education.' *Oxford Review of Education* 19.4, 527–46.

Norwich, B. (1997) *A Trend Towards Inclusion*. Bristol: Centre for Studies on Inclusive Education.

Office for Standards in Education (1998a) *The National Literacy Project*. London: OFSTED.

Office for Standards in Education (1998b) *The National Numeracy Project*. London: OFSTED.

Prais, S. (1993) *Economic Performance and Education*. London: NIESR.

Pringle, M. L. K., Butler, N. R. and Davie, R. (1966) *Eleven Thousand Seven Year Olds*. London: Longman.

Reynolds, D. and Farrell, S. (1996) *Worlds Apart? A Survey of International Comparisons of Educational Achievement Involving England*. London: HMSO.

Rutter, M., Tizard, J. and Whitmore, K. (1970) *Education, Health and Behaviour*. London: Longman.

Slee, R. (ed.) (1993) *Is There a Desk with my Name on it?* London: Falmer Press.

Special Educational Needs Tribunal (1995) *Annual Report 1994–95*. London: Special Educational Needs Tribunal.

Taylor Fitz-Gibbon, C. (1996) *Monitoring Education*. London: Cassell.

Thomas, G. and Davis, P. (1997) 'Special Needs: Objective Reality or Personal Construction? Judging Reading Difficulty after the Code of Practice.' *Educational Research* 39.3, 263–70.

Index